TEN YEARS IN THE WTO: HAS CHINA KEPT ITS PROMISES?

HEARING

BEFORE THE

CONGRESSIONAL-EXECUTIVE COMMISSION ON CHINA

ONE HUNDRED TWELFTH CONGRESS

FIRST SESSION

DECEMBER 13, 2011

Printed for the use of the Congressional-Executive Commission on China

Available via the World Wide Web: http://www.cecc.gov

U.S. GOVERNMENT PRINTING OFFICE

74–026 PDF   WASHINGTON : 2012

CONGRESSIONAL-EXECUTIVE COMMISSION ON CHINA

LEGISLATIVE BRANCH COMMISSIONERS

House

CHRISTOPHER H. SMITH, New Jersey,
  Chairman
FRANK WOLF, Virginia
DONALD A. MANZULLO, Illinois
EDWARD R. ROYCE, California
TIM WALZ, Minnesota
MARCY KAPTUR, Ohio
MICHAEL HONDA, California

Senate

SHERROD BROWN, Ohio, *Cochairman*
MAX BAUCUS, Montana
CARL LEVIN, Michigan
DIANNE FEINSTEIN, California
JEFF MERKLEY, Oregon
SUSAN COLLINS, Maine
JAMES RISCH, Idaho

EXECUTIVE BRANCH COMMISSIONERS

SETH D. HARRIS, Department of Labor
MARIA OTERO, Department of State
FRANCISCO J. SÁNCHEZ, Department of Commerce
KURT M. CAMPBELL, Department of State
NISHA DESAI BISWAL, U.S. Agency for International Development

PAUL B. PROTIC, *Staff Director*
LAWRENCE T. LIU, *Deputy Staff Director*

(II)

CONTENTS

STATEMENTS

APPENDIX

PREPARED STATEMENTS

SUBMISSION FOR THE RECORD

TEN YEARS IN THE WTO:
HAS CHINA KEPT ITS PROMISES?

TUESDAY, DECEMBER 13, 2011

CONGRESSIONAL-EXECUTIVE
COMMISSION ON CHINA,
Washington, DC.

The hearing was convened, pursuant to notice, at 2:34 p.m., in room 2211, Rayburn House Office Building, Representative Chris Smith, Chairman, presiding.

Also present: Senator Sherrod Brown; Representative Marcy Kaptur.

OPENING STATEMENT OF HON. CHRIS SMITH, A U.S. REPRESENTATIVE FROM NEW JERSEY; CHAIRMAN, CONGRESSIONAL-EXECUTIVE COMMISSION ON CHINA

Chairman SMITH. The Commission will come to order, and good afternoon to everybody.

Ten years ago this week, China acceded to the World Trade Organization [WTO]. Prior to that, the United States granted China permanent normal trade relations, or PNTR. This Commission was formed in that process with a mandate to monitor human rights and the development of the rule of law, or the lack of progress thereof, in China.

In 1998, two years before China joined the WTO, I chaired a hearing of the Subcommittee on International Operations and Human Rights of the Foreign Affairs Committee which examined whether bringing China into the WTO would improve its human rights record.

At the time, I noted reports from the State Department and Amnesty International citing serious problems in several key areas of China's human rights record, such as the imprisonment and abuse of prisoners of conscience, including those who sought genuine independent representation for China's workers, restrictions on religious freedom, and the implementation of coercive population control, including forced abortion and coercive organ harvesting, among other abuses.

As a member of the WTO, China has experienced tremendous economic growth and integration into the global economy. But as this Commission's most recent annual report documents, China continues to massively violate the basic human rights of its own people and systematically undermines the rule of law.

Lawyers and activists who stand up for individual rights are detained, often under deplorable conditions, and tortured. Chen Guangcheng, a blind, self-taught legal activist is imprisoned in his own home after spending time in prison. Both he and his wife had been beaten, often to the point of unconsciousness.

Nobel Laureate Liu Xiaobo continues to serve an 11-year prison sentence for peacefully advocating for political reform. Web sites that do not adhere to the government line are shut down. Freedom of religion is denied to those who worship outside of state-sanctioned institutions, and believers are systematically harassed, incarcerated, and tortured. Ethnic minorities are persecuted as well.

This hearing, asking whether China has kept its promises as a member of the WTO, will also revisit a hearing the Commission held in June 2002, six months after China joined the WTO. That hearing was titled, "WTO: Will China Keep Its Promises, and Can It?" There was optimism by some at the time, but even that was tempered by caution. China was liberalizing. It was a vast and promising market and foreign businesses were eager to see the imposition of the WTO's set of rules and principles bring some order to the Chinese investment and legal system.

It seemed at the time that China's leadership envisioned a market economy more similar to ours than that of a Communist state. However, some people, including me and some of our Commissioners, were highly skeptical that the Chinese WTO ascension would lead to the rule of law. Would China change the WTO or would the WTO change China? Judging by the expressions of the past 10 years, I think the answer to the first question, whether China has and will keep its promises, is sadly, no.

Arguably, the Chinese people now have more freedom to participate in China's changing economy, but the Chinese Government continues to place harsh restrictions on that participation. More Chinese citizens are able to travel, but many dissidents are barred from leaving the country.

The deplorable state of workers' rights in the PRC not only means that Chinese men, women, and children in the workforce are exploited and put at risk, but also that U.S. workers are severely hurt as well by profoundly unfair advantages that go to those corporations who benefit from China's heinous labor practices.

Human rights abuses abroad have the direct consequence of robbing Americans of their jobs and livelihoods here at home. Charlie Wowkanech, the president of the New Jersey State AFL–CIO, testified at my hearing in 1998. It was one of a series that we had in the late nineties on the WTO and human rights.

But at that particular one his words are as true today as what he said then. He said, "Chinese economic policy depends on maintenance of a strategy of aggressive exports and carefully restricted foreign access to its home market. They systematically violate internationally recognized workers' rights, and it's a strategically necessary component of that policy.

Chinese labor activists are regularly jailed or imprisoned in reeducation camps for advocating free and independent trade unions, for protesting corruption and embezzlement, for insisting that they be paid wages that they are owed—the so-called arrearage problem—and for talking to journalists about working conditions in China."

On the one hand, the Internet seemingly gives Chinese citizens greater access to information than was possible before, but it is heavily censored, restricting access by Chinese citizens to information about U.S. companies to the Chinese market. Moreover, the Internet has become a ubiquitous, potent weapon of suppression, employed with devastating impact.

In 2006, I held the first major hearing ever on Internet freedom in response to Yahoo's turning over the personally identifying information of an email account holder named Xier Tao to the Chinese Government, who tracked him down and sentenced him to 10 years for sending abroad emails that revealed the details of the Chinese Government's press controls.

At that hearing, Yahoo, Google, Microsoft, and Cisco testified as to what we might ruefully call their worst practices of cooperation with the Internet police of a totalitarian government, by China. Since then, China has further transformed what should have been a Freedom Plaza to Big Brother's best friend.

The technologies that the Chinese Government uses to track, monitor, block, filter, trace, remove, attack, hack, and remotely take over the Internet activity, content and end users has exploded.

Last week I introduced the Global Online Freedom Act, a bill that requires the State Department to beef up its reporting on Internet freedom in the annual country reports on human rights practices, and to identify by name Internet-restricting countries.

The bill requires Internet companies listed on the U.S. Stock Exchange to disclose to the Securities and Exchange Commission how they conduct their human rights due diligence, including with regard to the collection and sharing of personally identifiable information with repressive governments and the steps they take to notify users when they remove content or block access to content. That would, of course, cover Chinese corporations like Baidu and others who do business here in the United States and list on the Exchange.

Finally, in response to many reports that we have all seen in the papers recently of U.S. technology being used to track down or conduct surveillance of activists through the Internet or mobile devices, the barrier to prohibit the export of hardware or software that can be used for potentially illicit activity, such as surveillance, tracking, and blocking to the governments of Internet-restricting countries, especially China.

So could China have kept its promises of a decade ago? Of course it could have, though doing so would have meant the Chinese Communist Party would have had to submit to the rule of law. China faced many challenges when it joined the WTO, however, given its economic success and clout, as well as the immense resources it has poured into the expansion of the state's—on its economy, China certainly could have kept its promises if it had wished to do so.

So how is China doing by WTO standards? Awful. China has agreed to abide by the WTO principles of non-discrimination and transparency, however, U.S. exporters face many barriers when trying to sell products to China, starting with customs delays and other problems at the border. Those problems extend into China's markets.

4

Companies in the large and growing state-owned sector operate under a set of policies that favor Chinese producers. Also, it is extremely difficult for our companies to access government procurement.

Some of these barriers are obvious, such as China's indigenous innovation policy, which has created strong incentives to condition market access on the transfer of valuable technology, contrary to WTO rules.

Others, such as directed purchasing of China's main products by Chinese state-owned companies are harder to prove, notwithstanding China's agreements that state-owned companies would operate on a market basis.

There is no reciprocity—not strictly speaking a WTO requirement, but certainly a principle underlying the WTO. It is much more difficult for American companies to access the Chinese market than it is for Chinese companies to reach buyers in the United States. Even China's Internet censorship serves to keep American products and services out of the Chinese market, blocking access to China and U.S. Web sites, in many cases.

China's record of protection of intellectual property rights, a fundamental WTO obligation, is abysmal. Infringement of our companies' intellectual property [IP] leads to lost sales to China from the United States and other countries, lost royalty payments, and damaged reputations, and presents a risk to consumers here and in China of unwittingly buying counterfeit pharmaceuticals or unsafe, fake products.

The level playing field promised as part of China's WTO ascension has not arrived. WTO membership has resulted in a massive shift of jobs and wealth from the United States to China, which has come, again, at a huge cost to us.

Let us not forget the trade deficit is in China's favor and it has tripled over the past 10 years. In 2010, it was a whopping $273 billion. It also has come at a cost to the credibility of the WTO itself, raising the question: Is China killing the WTO? Given China's state capitalism and poor governance, the impact of China's failure to comply with WTO norms is compounded by the WTO's relative inability to deal effectively with a mercantilist state-directed economy such as China's. The WTO presupposes transparency and rule of law. These do not exist.

I'd like to yield now to Cochairman Sherrod Brown.

STATEMENT OF HON. SHERROD BROWN, A U.S. SENATOR FROM OHIO; COCHAIRMAN, CONGRESSIONAL–EXECUTIVE COMMISSION ON CHINA

Senator BROWN. Thank you, Mr. Chairman. A special thank you, Assistant U.S. Trade Representative Claire Reade. Thank you for joining us. We look forward to hearing your comments.

Ten years ago, this Commission grew out of the passage of PNTR in the House and Senate and signature from the President. This Commission was created to monitor human rights and rule of law in development in China. Today we're here to talk about what the last 10 years have meant. Chairman Smith, I think, outlined that well. We want to understand better whether we're better off, whether China's kept its promises, where we are headed.

At the time it joined the WTO, China made many promises. Chinese leaders pledged to reduce trade barriers and open up markets. They promised to increase transparency, to protect intellectual property rights, and to reform their legal system.

China's supporters, from CEOs to Members of the House and Senate, to editorial writers, argued that WTO membership would bring human rights and freedom and the rule of law into China, magically perhaps. Those of us on the other side of the spectrum, including my friend Wei Jingsheng, who is with us here today, raised serious doubts about China's WTO membership. We did not prevail.

Yet after 10 years it is clear that China is not living up to its promises or to the expectations, as unrealistic as many of us thought they were, or the expectations of its supporters. Far from becoming freer, the Chinese people are burdened with limited rights to basic freedoms of speech, religion, and assembly, and it's getting worse.

From the harsh crackdown on human rights lawyers and activists after the Arab Spring, to the brutal policies in Tibet that have led to a recent wave of self-immolations, China's Communist Party shows no signs of easing its tight grip on the Chinese people. There is no better example of this than Liu Xiaobo.

At this time last year Liu was being awarded the Nobel Peace Prize, but the dissident writer couldn't travel to Oslo to receive the award. He was stuck in a Chinese prison, another victim of a system that silences anyone who speaks out for human rights.

At last count, the Commission had documented some 1,500 cases of political prisoners in China, and those are just the ones we know about. Those are innocent people like Liu who are being punished for peacefully exercising fundamental human rights.

Not only did WTO not bring freedom and democracy to China, it so certainly didn't bring fair trade either. Instead, China has flouted WTO rules, rules which they said they would accept under the rule of law, and gamed the system to its unending advantage.

While China has chosen to comply with some WTO rules, overall the list of WTO violations is a long one: Rampant intellectual property theft; massive subsidies for China's exports; hoarding of rare earths and other raw materials. China has refused to commit to the WTO's agreement on government procurement. These violations not only show China's lack of respect for the rule of law, they also cost us dearly in lost American jobs and a stalled economic recovery.

U.S. intellectual property-intensive firms alone have lost almost $50 billion to intellectual property right violations, with those same firms reporting that better enforcement can lead to some 1 million new U.S. jobs. Some of the worst violations affect Ohio companies forced to compete against a country that manipulates its currency and subsidizes its manufacturers.

Given our own companies' well-founded fears of retaliation by Chinese regulators and companies if they speak up, we in government should be charged with the responsibility to give voice to their concerns. We know of petitions at ITC [U.S. International Trade Commission] and the Commerce Department where unions would petition and companies would be afraid to join those petitions because of potential retaliation in the business they are doing in China.

The most damaging of China's unfair trade practices is its currency manipulation. By deliberately holding down the value of its currency to boost exports, China has built the largest trade surplus in history, to the detriment of the United States and other trading partners. Currency manipulation provides an unfair subsidy to Chinese exports of up to 40 percent, by the estimate of some economists.

One of those economists is here today with us, Clyde Prestowitz, who has estimated that the percentage of the unfair subsidy to China is up to 40 percent. It practices the most protectionist policy of any major country since World War II, according to economist Fred Bergsten of the Peterson Institute.

Additionally, American manufacturers seeking to sell their products to China, our Nation's fastest-growing export market—from a fairly small base, I would add—are hit with the same percentage in what amounts to an unfair tariff. The advantages enjoyed by Chinese manufacturers cost American jobs not just in traditional industries like steel and autos and textiles, but jobs in wind, solar, and clean energy sectors, critical to our recovery.

There is no indication it will get better. In fact, China's state-owned sector is growing, further skewing the playing field in favor of China's heavily subsidized state-owned enterprises. With no end in sight, we have got to do something.

I applaud the U.S. Trade Representative for more aggressive efforts to challenge China in the WTO in everything from Internet censorship to raw materials. I look forward to hearing from Assistant U.S. Trade Representative Reade on her office's plans going forward. There is much more we can do.

That's why the Senate voted this fall to address currency manipulation by a resounding vote of 63 to 35. We passed the Currency Exchange Rate Oversight Reform Act of 2011, legislation I authored with several colleagues. It represents the biggest bipartisan jobs legislation the Senate has passed this year. I encourage the House to bring the currency bill to a vote. The House has passed that bill overwhelmingly in similar legislation from a couple of years ago.

American workers and American manufacturers can compete with anyone. Over the last 10 years though, China has sought to sidestep and reshape the WTO to benefit China at our expense. That is not competing, that's cheating. We must act now while we still have a chance.

Thank you, Mr. Chairman.

Representative SMITH. Chairman Brown, thank you very much.

I'd like to now introduce and thank Claire Reade, who is Assistant U.S. Trade Representative for China Affairs at the Office of the U.S. Trade Representative [USTR]. She is responsible for developing and implementing U.S. trade policy toward China, Hong Kong, Macau, Taiwan, and Mongolia. Previously, Ms. Reade served as Chief Counsel for China Trade Enforcement at USTR in the beginning of 2006.

Before joining USTR, Ms. Reade was a senior partner at Arnold & Porter, where she was an international trade litigator and counselor. Thank you so very much for being here today and we look forward to your testimony.

STATEMENT OF CLAIRE READE, ASSISTANT U.S. TRADE REP-RESENTATIVE FOR CHINA AFFAIRS, OFFICE OF THE U.S. TRADE REPRESENTATIVE

Ms. READE. Thank you very much. Chairman Smith, Chairman Brown, I appreciate very much the opportunity to testify today on China's efforts to fulfill the commitments it made when it joined the WTO 10 years ago. This is a matter of great priority for the administration and for U.S. Trade Representative, Ambassador Ron Kirk.

When China acceded to the WTO, China's leaders took many impressive steps to implement a set of sweeping reforms in order to meet its commitments. These steps unquestionably strengthened both China's rule of law and the economic reforms that China had begun in 1978. Trade and investment also expanded dramatically, providing substantial opportunities for U.S. businesses, workers, farmers, and service suppliers, and a wealth of affordable goods for U.S. consumers.

Despite this progress, the overall picture of China's actions to implement its WTO commitments remains complex, given a troubling trend in China toward intensified state intervention in the Chinese economy over the last five years.

In short, even with the tremendous progress that China has made in the complex task of implementing its WTO commitments, critical work remains. Today I want to highlight four areas that continue to cause particular concern for the United States. For more details, I would refer the Commission to the 2011 USTR Report on China's WTO Compliance that was issued yesterday by the USTR, and I will submit a copy of this for the record.

The first area I want to focus on is effective enforcement of intellectual property rights in China. This remains a massive challenge. Counterfeiting and piracy in particular remain at unacceptably high levels in China and trade secret theft is also becoming very worrisome.

Second, China's pursuit of an array of industrial policies raises serious concerns. Subsidies and other discriminatory policies benefit state-owned enterprises, as well as other favored companies.

Third, even though China is now the United States' largest agricultural export market, this massive and beneficial trade does not flow as smoothly as it should, given problems with regulatory transparency and predictability.

Finally, even though the United States continues to enjoy a substantial surplus in trade and services with China and the market for U.S. service suppliers remains promising, China's discriminatory regulatory processes and other similar problems frustrate efforts of foreign suppliers to achieve their full market potential in China. Going forward, Ambassador Kirk will continue to vigorously pursue increased benefits for U.S. stakeholders in all of these areas.

Let me turn, now, to another important area: transparency. This is one of the core principles of the WTO agreement and is reflected throughout China's WTO accession commitments. These commitments required a profound shift in Chinese policies and China did make important strides to improve transparency. Nevertheless, it appears that China still has more work to do.

Three areas of remaining work stand out. First, China committed to publish all of its trade-related laws, regulations, and other measures. While China has complied in many respects, it still does not appear that China publishes all its measures.

Second, China committed to published trade-related measures for public comment before implementation. China has made important improvements in this area, but some agencies continue to promulgate final measures with little or no opportunity for public comment.

Third, China committed to make its trade-related measures available in one or more WTO languages, but it appears China has made very limited progress in implementing this commitment.

The administration will continue to push China to undertake further necessary steps to improve transparency. China's WTO membership offers an important tool for managing the increasingly complex U.S.-China trade relationship.

A common WTO rulebook and an impartial body in Geneva have helped the two sides resolve differences and the United States has not hesitated to pursue its rights with China through WTO dispute settlement. In the last three years alone, the United States has brought five cases to the WTO on wind power subsidies, misuse of trade remedy law, discriminatory barriers in the service sector, and trade-distortive export restraints.

These disputes, combined with the enforcement work we pursue in the Joint Commission on Commerce and Trade, the Strategic and Economic Dialogue, and other trade tools, including Special 301, help try to ensure that U.S. stakeholders derive the full promise of China's WTO membership.

The importance of the WTO to the U.S.-China relationship highlights the fact that for China itself there is a critical stake in strengthening the WTO system. That means, for example, that at the upcoming WTO ministerial in Geneva, China should join in to help solve the Doha Round impasse and implement meaningful trade liberalization and credible trade rules to govern the WTO's system in the future.

Thank you very much for the opportunity to testify today. I look forward to hearing your questions.

[The report is retained in Commission files.]

[The prepared statement of Ms. Reade appears in the appendix.]

Senator BROWN [presiding]. Thank you, Ms. Reade, very much.

Let me start with one of the points you just made about the five WTO cases against China since Ambassador Kirk assumed his position, I believe in March 2009. There were some seven cases filed in the many more years than that prior to his taking that position. There are a number of us in the Senate and the House who have fought for more money for trade enforcement who would like to see a more aggressive USTR, not just on China issues with WTO and bilaterally, but with other countries, too.

But speak, if you would. Does this increased frequency from seven cases over a several-year period to five cases in less than two-and-a-half years, does that reflect a change in the way the

United States perceives China's role in the WTO, and is that something we can expect to continue, in your view?

Ms. READE. I think it's very clear that this administration has made enforcement a top priority, and that includes enforcement with regard to our rights vis-a-vis China. So not only do we have the five WTO cases that you mentioned, but we are the first administration to implement remedies in response to a Section 421 petition on Chinese tire imports, as well as the first administration to accept a Section 301 petition against China since China joined the WTO, which led, as you probably are aware, to the WTO case on wind power subsidies.

So I think there's no question that this is a high priority and that the administration is extremely committed to ensuring that we enforce our rights vigorously in the WTO.

When China first joined the WTO one could say that it took a watch-and-wait approach as it became more familiar with the WTO, so I think its role has changed over time. I would say this actually shows up both in China's dispute settlement activities and in its role in the Doha Round.

I would say with regard to dispute settlement, we have no problem dealing with China's legitimate complaints. In fact, China brought a complaint against our use of the Section 421 mechanism and the WTO completely vindicated our rights to impose those import tariffs on tires.

We have seen troubling evidence of China increasing its intervention in the economy, and we have responded accordingly in our enforcement efforts, both against state-owned enterprises, for example, the pending electronic payments case, as well as a number of cases on troubling subsidies brought by China. So I would say that we are intensifying our efforts. This is a very important tool and we need to use it to its fullest.

Senator BROWN. Thank you.

The 421 case on tires had several interesting aspects, starting with the petitioner, the United Steelworkers, formerly the Rubber Workers—they are now part of the Steelworkers. It's a company headquartered in Findlay, Ohio. What was interesting is that the company did not join in the petition for reasons, perhaps, of potential retribution on their operations in China.

We know that the company didn't specifically say, to my knowledge, what all the reasons were that they were not part of that petition, but I think it speaks to the issue of the Chinese willing to intimidate and perhaps deny various kinds of services or business in China if they enter those kinds of cases.

I would also add that after that decision was made, within a matter of days, I recall—weeks, certainly, it seems days—that Cooper Tire hired about 100 more steelworkers in Findlay because clearly the Chinese were dumping tires before that.

You mentioned 301. Before I get to a question about 301, let me ask a pretty simple question. During the whole PNTR process, one of the things we talked about was not just the differential in wages between China and the United States, but the whole issue of labor rights. Labor rights were not obviously considered in WTO accession for China. Has the absence of labor standards made it more difficult to level the playing field?

Ms. READE. The issue of labor rights is incredibly important and it's one that has to be dealt with using all of the tools that we have available. You are correct in indicating that the WTO framework does not deal directly with labor rights, however the U.S. Trade Representative's Office participates in several fora where these issues are dealt with. One is the labor dialogue, which also involves our Labor Department, which is an important venue for dealing with some of these issues.

In addition, we participate in the human rights dialogue, which is led by the State Department, which also deals with these questions. I think there is no question that this was part of the reason why your Commission was created and that it's extremely important to continue to air these issues.

The U.S. Trade Representative, in its own lane, is taking actions that are designed to ensure a level playing field. First, the issues of rule of law and transparency are extremely important. Issues of non-discrimination are also very important.

The 12 WTO cases that we have taken against China, accepting and acting upon a Section 301 petition, and imposing remedies in response to a Section 421 petition, I think, are all testaments to the fact that we don't hesitate to use WTO dispute settlement and other enforcement tools in addition to bilateral dialogue, because there are instances when China has been willing to resolve situations without going to the WTO. The array of trade challenges with China are definitely things that we are working on night and day and that require all of our efforts together, and we welcome your continued help.

Senator BROWN. Thank you.

You mentioned at the beginning of your answer to that question about labor rights, you said, "with all the tools we have available." What tools do you wish you had available to enforce labor rights?

Ms. READE. I think——

Senator BROWN. Whether it's ILO standards or wherever your answer takes you.

Ms. READE [continuing]. I will have to defer that to the Labor Department, and to the extent it's human rights, to the State Department, that lead those dialogues because I think they are better positioned to answer that.

Senator BROWN. Okay. Fair enough.

I want to talk about Section 301. Over the years, Members of Congress and groups of industry and unions have petitioned the USTR and China on labor rights, economic issues, currency issues, all kinds of things.

The Bush administration, as you may remember, dismissed, I thought amazingly and perhaps infamously, the labor position in a matter of hours when some unions—I think it was the AFL—had offered petitions to USTR and China's currency manipulation in 2005 and 2007.

In a 301 investigation, USTR seeks consultation with the trading partner, which we would hope would resolve in a settlement, or USTR then would initiate a more formal process. There is broad discretion as to what that action might be, as you know, whether it's a case at the WTO or whether it's imposing duties.

As you also know, a 301 can be self-initiated by an administration. I won't ask you whether you think China manipulates its currency, I think there's no question. The last three or more presidential administrations notwithstanding, I think it's pretty clear they do manipulate currency. But I won't ask you that question.

We're waiting on the Treasury Department again to submit to Congress its biennial report on that issue, but I'm not holding my breath. It continues to amaze me that an administration that cares about what this one says it does would not do that, but that's another issue.

Let me ask it this way. How would a Section 301 petition on currency be received if that were filed with USTR today?

Ms. READE. Other countries' currency policies are the responsibility of the U.S. Treasury Department within the administration. What I can say on the currency issue is that both President Obama and Secretary Geithner have said that China's progress to date is insufficient and that China needs to do more.

Senator BROWN. If there were petitions submitted—I'm not going to let you get off quite that easy, but nice try. And I appreciate your input on this and I know you're in a difficult position. But if this petition were received, the Section 301 petition were sent to you, how would the decisionmaking process work at USTR? Is this a decision that would be—can you answer that, even? But give me your thoughts on that.

Ms. READE. Yes. I'm not sure I'm in a position to answer the question, unfortunately, because I'm not the person in charge of Section 301 at USTR, that is the office of general counsel. Second, it obviously very much depends on what the petition is as to what happens. So unfortunately I'm not going to be able to be helpful.

Senator BROWN. Why do you think 301 is not utilized more? Do you think that outside groups don't utilize it much because of its sort of wholesale rejection or almost unthinking rejection at times in the history of the USTR? Do you think it's not seen as effective? Do you think that groups think it's futile? Not the self-initiated 301, but 301 coming from petitioners.

Ms. READE. Let me say two things on that. First of all, this administration is the administration that accepted a 301 petition, for the first time since China came into the WTO. So I think it's clear that this administration has a positive view toward the role that Section 301 can play.

I think if you look at what happened through the Section 301 petition you also see that it led to a WTO complaint and to resolution of a problem on a very serious subsidy in wind. It also resulted in progress at the JCCT [Joint Commission on Commerce and Trade], where we got another problematic wind-related provision removed, as China recognized the problem. I have little doubt that the Section 301 petition assisted in that.

The other initiative that I would tie to this situation is the work that was done to do the counter-notification in the World Trade Organization, where the United States notified more than 200 subsidies that China had not notified to the WTO, and a number of these were also in the clean energy sector.

There is no question that there is a positive role to be played, and you can see the kinds of efforts that the administration has taken when a Section 301 petition is accepted.

Senator BROWN. How did USTR know about those 200-plus subsidies? What's the process to identify those and research those and identify them as a problem, research them and be able to conclusively say they're subsidies?

Ms. READE. There are a number of routes that are taken. We use our own resources, both inside USTR—it's a very small agency—as well as the other agencies in the administration. As you know, the Department of Commerce is tasked with investigating potential subsidies, so that is another source of information for us. They also have an obligation to create a library of subsidy practices.

In addition, we use our very able embassy colleagues in Beijing, and we cannot do without our stakeholders. We take eyes and ears from everywhere in order to work on these problems.

Senator BROWN. How important is it in that panoply or array of places you get input from—sorry to mix a metaphor there—how important is it that companies or unions come forward and say "We think this is a subsidy?" Is that a major part of the information you get?

Ms. READE. It's extremely important to get the facts. That's the key—I'm putting my former lawyer hat on—because that is what allows you to take action when you have a basis for doing so.

Senator BROWN. I'm not suggesting that a company or union come forward and say this is a problem and you're immediately going to say, oh, that's a fact, we'll move. I'm saying, do you find out about these subsidies in part because a company in Brunswick, Ohio, or a company in Toledo says I think they're cheating, can you look into this? Is that a big part of what you get?

Ms. READE. I would say it is a very valuable contribution. I can give you an example. We had a case at the WTO on famous export brands and some of the work on that actually came up from concerns that textile organizations had and that they brought to our attention. We also have had steel industry folks come to us with their concerns.

Outside of the subsidies area, I can tell you that the issues of export restraints on raw materials is an area where stakeholders have come to us and helped us put the beads on the necklace to realize that this was a cross-cutting policy that was having a major effect on our stakeholders. So it's definitely a very valuable contribution.

Senator BROWN. Are you more likely to hear from a trade association, an individual company, or a union?

Ms. READE. I don't think that there's one organization or another that we're more likely to hear from. I would say that when you have an organization that has resources that are devoted to trying to track certain issues, that you obviously are going to be able to get more detailed information from that organization. So it is when organizations are committed to looking at issues, for example, like transparency or indigenous innovation or particular subsidies, that you will get the benefits of their research.

Senator BROWN. Do you make any effort—we try to in our State. Chris Slevin, sitting behind me, one of his jobs is to work with companies and if they see problems, help sort of funnel those issues that we can analyze. As good as Chris is, we don't have the staff or expertise to do what you can do on the ground in Beijing, and all that.

So we do some proactive, "Please come to us and tell us if you see problems and we will help you prove it or find out it's not true." Do you do that kind of proactive work at USTR? If the answer is "a bit," or "yes," or "we'd like to do more"—we hope some of the additional funding we're trying to get you will help you do that— is there an effort? Is that a charge from Ambassador Kirk that you have a responsibility to do?

Ms. READE. We make as much of an effort as we can to be proactive in trying to look at possible issues. I should have added the Congress to the list of sources where we get important information. The input that we get from your constituents coming in and the information from your offices directly is extremely helpful to us.

In addition, we are very grateful for the resources that are in the President's budget to enhance the efforts that we make. Right now, we are working around the clock to try to identify the problems we face with China, so it's something we take incredibly seriously. We welcome your assistance and your support.

Senator BROWN. Would it make sense for you to go to trade associations, particularly in industries that you suspect might be losing jobs and market share because of foreign competition that might or might not be fair? Would it make sense for the USTR to have a program to go to those trade association meetings and work with those industries and have them—encourage them to come forward and talk to you about any of those potential problems?

Ms. READE. We have a great deal of interaction with our stakeholders. We have it through the Joint Commission on Commerce and Trade [JCCT] process. For example, the JCCT is a year-round process and we start that every year with meetings with stakeholders and as many industry associations as we can get together with to identify both WTO problems and problems that may not be, as well as challenging issues that we may be able to resolve before they become WTO problems. So that is an integral part of what it is we do.

I should also indicate that prior to issuing our WTO compliance report to Congress every year we ask for input from all stakeholders, including a Federal Register notice asking for submissions and testimony at a public hearing that we hold, as well as a range of followup activities. So we are doing the best we can. We can always do more and we welcome your ideas about that.

Senator BROWN. I have one. I would like to ask you to encourage my colleagues, as I try to do, but you can do it from a more official, nonpartisan, outside way—or inside way, too, for that matter—to urge Members of Congress to work with you on that in a proactive sort of way.

I don't think most Members of Congress think a lot—I mean, some of us worked on trade issues in China longer than others, just an issue we chose to work on. People have some entrepreneurial spirit around here in the sense of what they decide to do.

But in any sort of constructive, methodical way that you can encourage House and Senate Members to encourage their businesses to come forward to help us enforce these trade laws—I mean, I could rattle off, which I do ad nauseam, probably, companies in Ohio that have done better and have done significant hiring because of enforcement that the Obama administration has done.

While I don't think that you are aggressive enough as an administration, I don't think that your position on trade is always where it should be, I think you've been better than at least the last three or four of either party on enforcement of trade law and we want to continue to push you. Anything you can do to get my colleagues to enter that fray would be helpful.

Ms. READE. Thank you. I made a note, and we'll definitely follow up.

Senator BROWN. Good. Thank you.

And I apologize for this. I will call a short recess until Chairman Smith comes back and then we'll continue. If you can remain a few more minutes, Ms. Reade, and then the second panel also can. I apologize for that. Thanks.

[Whereupon, at 3:15 p.m. the hearing was recessed.]

AFTER RECESS [3:24 P.M.]

Chairman SMITH [presiding]. The Commission will come to order.

I have a few questions and I thank you for your willingness to stay. We did have four votes on the floor of the House, so I apologize again.

I know Senator Brown asked a few questions relative to workers' rights, and I would like to ask specifically, what efforts has USTR undertaken, or will undertake, to investigate labor rights violations in China? You might recall back on June 8, 2006, I co-signed a 301 petition that was written by Mark Barenberg, Professor of Law at Columbia, on behalf of the AFL–CIO.

Frankly, it was one of the finest bits of investigative reporting, and in terms of the petition it was very heavily footnoted and I think got to a lot of the issues with regard to worker rights violations that have not really been focused upon anywhere sufficiently enough.

For example, number six of the petition talks about the pattern of denying workplace rights and standards, denial of free association and rights of collective bargaining, the sub-class of migrant factory workers, bonded labor. Failure to provide standards for minimum wages and maximum hours. Failure to provide standards for occupational safety and health.

I would note parenthetically, he points out in this that even the government reports large numbers of people who die every year. I think the number he puts in there is close to 130,000, and that's the reported figure, because there is no such thing as OSHA [Occupational Safety and Health Administration] in the PRC. Failure to provide child labor standards. Failure to enforce rights against forced labor in the penal system. It goes on and on with, again, heavily documented, heavily footnoted information.

I remember asking USTR at the time, and we actually had a Foreign Affairs Committee hearing and I lifted up the petition which I had signed onto—Ben Cardin and I were the two, and the AFL–

CIO, John Sweeney and Richard Trumka, secretary and treasurer of the AFL–CIO—and asked that at least an investigation be initiated and we were told no, that it would not happen. It seems to me that the barest minimal action should be to undertake an investigation like this.

I meet with people involved with trade in China all the time. Even though they know my position with regard to human rights, many are very empathetic. I would just note parenthetically that Google was against the Global Online Freedom Act for the first year after I introduced it. It was a different version, but it was still so named.

They came around and actually supported it because they finally realized they weren't opening up China, they were unwittingly closing it down. I've always argued there are two things necessary for a dictatorship to survive and prosper, propaganda and secret police, and certainly the Internet aided and abetted both of those parts of that equation.

So I would ask you, I plan on doing a formal letter to USTR, asking that an unfair labor practice be investigated vis-a-vis labor issues. We will be sending that letter over to your office very shortly. Hopefully some other Members—and I'm sure—will sign on. But it just seems, in a time when—in this report, the wages at 10 to 50 cents per hour, the wage issue where people don't even get paid, despite all of it there are all these wildcat strikes, as you know, and people suffer. The iron fist comes down.

I've had hearings in the past where we had labor rights activists who were not going back, they had gotten asylum, tell how despite all of this they would still try to organize and achieve what the ILO would recognize as a minimum standard for labor rights.

So I would ask you, please, to undertake an investigation. We'll do the letters, if you need additional push, as a Commission. But it seems to me this is an idea whose time has come. I met a man in New Jersey who was doing business in China, and he said when he got over there it was kind of like a company fair that China had put on.

He got to talking to the Chinese leadership who were part of this effort and they got into wages, and what do I pay my salaried employees. They said, don't worry about it. For every one person, you can pay them the barest minimum because if that person doesn't want the job there's 99 in line that will take the job for a mere pittance.

Again, no occupational protections whatsoever in many cases— not all certainly, but many. So it seems to me, as I said in my opening, how does our laborers, since foreign sourcing has become the—and you even said yourself that things have gotten worse in the last five years. There seems to be a deterioration. As they gin up even more on their exports, more people will be exploited.

We all know if we're reading the papers, people are out on the streets, they get incarcerated, and they get beaten. And let's not forget, where did freedom come from? The trade unions and solidarity. Lech Walesa, the great leader in Poland. This is the linchpin, I think. So if you could undertake an investigation into labor exploitation as an unfair labor practice.

Ms. READE. Thank you very much, Congressman. This is an incredibly important issue and the work that you're doing on it to make it evident and to speak about it is very important. This administration believes this is an incredibly important issue and wants to take all avenues that are appropriate.

This is a human rights issue and the State Department has the lead. We also can address many of these issues in the labor dialogue, a recent innovation, with China, led by the Labor Department. It is also, as I had mentioned earlier, a very important reason why this Commission was brought into being.

So we think this is an incredibly important issue and are very appreciative of your continuing to air your concerns. I obviously will take back your concerns to the USTR and make sure to inform Ambassador Kirk.

Chairman SMITH. I appreciate that. Because at the time we were told they wouldn't. Again, I don't care who's in the White House. This was during the Bush administration and I'm a Republican. It was very critical and the USTR would not, or failed to even initiate a preliminary investigation.

So I would hope, barest minimum, begin that investigation because this is Pandora's Box. As this gets opened up, we realize how cruelly exploited these people are. I would note parallel to this, since the days of George H.W. Bush and then was carried over into Clinton, carried over into George W. Bush, the whole idea of gulag labor, which is in violation of Smoot-Hawley, I can't tell you how many times over the years the administrations have trotted out, "Oh, but we have an MOU [memorandum of understanding] with the PRC on importing goods made by prison labor." It sounds good on paper, but it's a Swiss cheese agreement, filled with huge, gaping holes.

I've met with our Customs people every time I go to China in Beijing, wonderful Customs agents, and they are like the Maytag repairman because the way it reads, unless we have actionable information that we then give to the Chinese, they investigate, they tell us what they find and then we act from there. Good luck getting the Chinese Government, that makes money hand-over-fist from exploitation, to actually do it.

So I know this is a State Department issue, but it's related to the unfair labor. As Harry Wu and Wei Jingsheng and so many others have pointed out, so many parts get produced in these factories with political prisoners, Falun Gong, Christians, Tibetans, all being reduced to slave labor and it ends up on our shelves.

I would note parenthetically that Frank Wolf and I, right after Tiananmen Square, got into Beijing Prison Number One. While we were there we took some jelly shoes—we asked. We didn't steal them. We took them from Warden Jo, who actually said, okay, you can have them—and some socks that were being exported to the United States. He wondered why we wanted jelly shoes. They were the big craze, you might recall, back in the early 1990s.

Sure enough, there were 40 Tiananmen Square activists in that prison camp, all with shaved heads. They looked like concentration camp victims that you would find in Nazi Germany or anywhere else. Although they weren't being killed, they were being exploited to the point of exhaustion, though. They wouldn't let us talk to them, but we did take back the shoes.

Well, we gave them to Commerce and an import ban was put on that because we had verifiable information about its origin. It seems to me we need to revisit the whole MOU issue because so many products are being made, nobody knows how many, that end up on our shelves, being made by gulag labor. So I plan on a separate hearing on that, either in my subcommittee or here in the Commission, shortly because the time has come to end that practice.

So I would ask you to factor that in, bring that back if you would, because these things are showing up on our shores and we had no idea what the proof of origin is, but we certainly can be suspect about it.

Did you want to comment on the MOU at all, or not?

Ms. READE. No. You asked me to take it back and I'm making a note to be sure that I remember to take it back. It's another area that is incredibly important, and we really appreciate your keeping it in the spotlight.

Chairman SMITH. Let me just ask you, recently the USTR had requested, through the WTO, information on China's Internet censorship. Has the PRC responded to the United States? Do you foresee a case against China concerning that censorship? And again, I applaud you for initiating that in the first place.

Ms. READE. Because it's the WTO where we are looking at the trade and investment implications of China's policies, the purpose of this request was to respond to problems that our small- and medium-sized enterprises have had where their opportunities to provide services into China have been frustrated by having their Web sites blocked for reasons that they can't understand.

So the purpose of this set of questions was to try to gain insight into what was going on and try to solve the problem. So in the first instance, that's what we're really trying to accomplish.

China has provided a response recently and we think it is going to require followup, but at least it's the opening of an avenue for dialogue. We are hopeful that we will be able to deal with this problem effectively and eliminate the barriers facing our small- and medium-sized enterprises who are having enough difficulty in these economic times.

Chairman SMITH. Thank you.

Let me just ask you, Wei Jingsheng will be testifying on the next panel, and I do hope you take his testimony and perhaps even stay to hear it. But I first met Wei in the early 1990s when he was let out of the gulag to get the Olympics in 2000.

He was that high of a value of political dissident that they thought one man would be sufficient to overcome human rights concerns to procure the Olympics in 2000. We had dinner together very openly. I mean, there are fewer people who are as brave and courageous as this man. He was then rounded up after he met with me and interrogated once again and was re-arrested when Olympics 2000 didn't go the way of the Chinese.

As you know, he's the father of the Democracy Web Movement. He was beaten severely, almost to the point of death, and then was finally, through a lot of the efforts on our government's side, the

U.S. Government, got freedom here in the United States, rested up, healed all the broken bones and all the other problems he had, and then came to my hearing on December 18, 1995, and just said things that I will never forget.

He said, "You Americans don't understand it. When you kowtow, when you are less than tough, transparent, look them in the eye and mean what you say and say what you mean, they take that as weakness, but they also beat us more in the laogai system. When you're tough, we see it with the guards. We always know how the Americans in particular, the Europeans to a lesser extent, are behaving vis-a-vis human rights, and that would include labor rights of course, by how they beat us in the prisons." I have never forgotten that. I've run that by other survivors of the laogai, including Harry Wu and many, many others, and they all say the same thing, that weakness is perceived as putting the imprimatur on cruelty to the dissidents and everyone else, and that would include labor rights activists.

Wei says that the Chinese Government continues naked trade protection measures. Do you agree with that? That's brought from his testimony.

Ms. READE. As I said in my testimony, there definitely are areas where China has critical work left to do. They include areas such as favoritism toward state-owned enterprises and discriminatory subsidies, and service sectors where they are blocking our companies from participating in China's market. That's what you see reflected in the WTO compliance efforts that we've been making.

That's why we have had five WTO disputes in the last three years. That's why we took the 421 actions that we took to impose remedies on the imports of Chinese tires, and that's why we accepted the Section 301 petition, the first administration to do that since China joined the WTO. It's precisely for those reasons, trying to respond to that. We are absolutely dedicated to continuing to vigorously enforcing U.S. trade rights whenever we see that kind of protectionism.

Chairman SMITH. Let me just ask one final question. Again, I thank you for your forbearance with the interruptions. Recently I held another hearing on the demographic winter that will overtake China in the not-too-distant future. Because of the one-child-per-couple policy, in effect since 1979, there are missing at least 100 million girls as a result of that gendercide.

We had testimony in this Commission just recently where we heard from the woman who wrote Bare Branches, a heavily footnoted book, something that the Pentagon needs to be reading as well as diplomats, that by 2020, 37 to 50 million men will not be able to find wives in China because they've been systematically eliminated through sex selection abortion. It's ongoing. There's no sign of abatement whatsoever.

There is talk sometimes, but certainly talk is cheap in Beijing and in Washington. It has just not shown any fruit whatsoever. There's even a group called All Girls Allowed, run by the great Chai Ling, trying to push governments, including Beijing, to stop its persecution of baby girls.

The other side, too, of the equation is the missing children. They have a population increase, as does the world, but it's all about longevity, not about births and about children. I've seen data that suggests that there's going to be a huge implosion in a decade, decade and a half.

I wonder how the Trade Representative, how our policy integrates the fact that China is heading toward ominous times because of a labor shortage that no one will acknowledge now, although there are some demographers in Beijing who do, but they are more aware than not.

I'm wondering if our trade policy—and I would say our military as well, but that wouldn't be your purview—incorporates that concern because China all of a sudden will find itself, I think, imploding because it'll have a senior population that is unsustainable vis-a-vis its worker population. Is that something that you're looking at very carefully, incorporating into our policy vis-a-vis China?

Ms. READE. You raise a fascinating aspect of China's policy choices. That's obviously not directly in the trade lane, but as you point out it has implications for the society and the economy. We are always trying to understand the fundamentals underneath China's economy as we are formulating our trade and economic policies, and I have made a note to see what our experts are thinking about that. Thank you very much.

Chairman SMITH. I appreciate that. If you'd like, we'll get you some of the latest hearing record. We had four learned demographers at one hearing, and it wasn't just on China, but even places like Russia. Nicholas Eberstadt from the American Enterprise Institute testified that in Russia, for the last 16 years, there have been 3 deaths for every 2 births, an unsustainable situation for Russia. He said by 2050, they'll have half the army. By the end of the century, they'll have half the country. China, despite the caricature that's painted of a bulging population, will have the same lack of children. The economic implications are huge for the United States and the world, not to mention China.

Ms. Kaptur?

STATEMENT OF HON. MARCY KAPTUR, A U.S. REPRESENTATIVE FROM OHIO; MEMBER, CONGRESSIONAL–EXECUTIVE COMMISSION ON CHINA

Representative KAPTUR. Thank you very much. Thank you, Mr. Chairman. I am sorry to be a little bit late in joining here. I want to thank Representative Reade for being with us today. As with the Chairman today, I wanted to raise the issue—I want to focus on the economy and the economic relations with China.

Obviously the hearing, has China kept its promises to the WTO, in my opinion the answer is an unmistakable no. Before China was granted permanent—I even hesitate to use the word "normal" trade relations. I had a problem with that when it was originally debated here in the Congress because it's anything but normal. It's a very abnormal relationship.

President Clinton argued, "The agreement will create unprecedented opportunities for American farmers, workers, and companies to compete successfully in China's market." Well, today the trade deficit with China is mammoth. Last year, our total trade deficit was over a half a trillion dollars globally, but over half of that, $273 billion was with one country: China.

Since PNTR was passed, over my objections, our total cumulative trade deficit with them was over $2 trillion. Two trillion dollars. A lot of people around here keep talking about the U.S. deficit and why our economy is not growing fast enough.

Well, if you study recent history you can see. You can almost track directly where that wealth creation has gone, which markets are open and which markets are not open. Now, in many places, including the state that I represent, you can see money, people, and jobs literally flowing out of our country and you can watch the trains pass as they're bringing in containers full of Chinese merchandise. Those containers are stacked all the way around the Great Lakes.

Dr. Clyde Prestowitz, who is testifying today, has estimated that every billion dollars in trade deficit translates to about 15,000 lost U.S. jobs. As I calculate the math, that means our country has lost over 4 million jobs just in recent history to China.

For the people that I represent, job creation is their number-one priority. In fact, we have to create 28 million jobs in our country between now and 2018 to employ all Americans who want a job. That is why this Commission, since its creation, I think, has a very important mandate, and quite frankly, opening up the Chinese market and getting some type of transparency, in my opinion, is extraordinarily important.

Now, I'm going to put some facts in the record, and I won't go through all this, Mr. Chairman, but the promises that U.S. manufactured products will gain real access to the Chinese market have never been kept. I'm going to give a couple of examples of that.

One example that the New York Times reported on earlier this month, and I ask that the entire article be placed in the record, stated that a Jeep Grand Cherokee in China costs $85,000. That's about three times what it costs in this country. Why is that? According to the New York Times it is due to a clever and obvious set of protective tariffs.

What have we done about that? Well, in Toledo, Ohio, which I represent, we make the Jeep Wrangler and I expect this Commission to take the issue of China's treatment of the U.S. auto industry seriously and to push our Trade Representatives to get a fair playing field. I would very much ask the U.S. Trade Representative's Office to develop a comprehensive strategy for addressing China's anti-competitive behavior.

In the region that I represent also we've been looking very hard at creating new energy systems, including solar, where we are now one of the three leading platforms in the country. We are not next to Stanford and we are not next to MIT, but we are next to major silicate and sand deposits and a history of glass production that lends our region well to compete in this market.

However, one domestic solar manufacturer has argued for some time that the Chinese are dumping photovoltaic cells on the U.S. market, and the recent U.S. International Trade Commission ruling in favor of the U.S. industry confirms it. I am going to ask that this Commission follow up on this issue and make it clear to the administration that we demand strong action in response.

Everywhere I look, it's the same story. Dr. Pat Choate testified before this Commissioner earlier this year and said China is the world's leading infringer of U.S.-owned patents, copyrights, trademarks, and trade secrets, and noted in his testimony the challenge is beyond the capacity of the Office of the U.S. Trade Representative to address.

We need to take the failure of China to live up to its commitment much more seriously, and I can guarantee you that if a company locates there in the solar industry, there are requirements that the Chinese Government places on them to produce—to co-produce, I should say—and to own a majority share of whatever investment is made there or to require that the company give away some of its independence in order to sell its product in the Chinese market.

This is a very different arrangement than we had been used to dealing with with other major industrial powers. I found it very interesting, Mr. Chairman, and I will end with this. A couple of years ago I asked several economists who were testifying before this Commission, what kind of system is this that creates such imbalances, that is not a fair playing field, that doesn't have transparency, that has very irregular trading and investment rules? What kind of an economic system would you call that?

The witnesses that day, 3 out of 4 on the panel, said we would call it "market Leninism." I said, you know, that's an expression I haven't heard before. I just place that on the record again today because it is a very different system than we are used to dealing with.

I would like to ask you, do you feel in your capacity that you actually have the power to address any of the concerns that I have noted, the trade imbalance, the investment requirements that the Chinese place on investment there, the theft of intellectual property, that you really have the ability to address that as USTR or do you think that's the responsibility of some entity in our government or the WTO itself?

[The article appears in the appendix.]

Ms. READE. China represents a massive challenge, for the reasons you have cited as well as for a number of others. I will say that the Obama administration is committed to a comprehensive trade strategy with China and USTR spends nights, days, weekends working as hard and creatively as we can to deal with those challenges.

I will say that we do have some tools at our disposal that I think are effective. At the WTO, we brought five cases in the last three years. Overall, the United States has brought 12 WTO cases against China, including cases that deal with these kinds of investment restrictions that you were referring to in certain sectors, as well as unfair subsidies and problems with IP standards in China.

Is it enough? Have we solved the problem? The points that you make indicate that there is a lot of work that remains to be done. But I can promise you that the work that we aim to do as an administration, we will be as dedicated and as intelligent in trying to use the tools at our disposal to do that. In addition to the WTO rules, I will tell you that we also have the Joint Commission on Commerce and Trade.

We just finished meetings in Beijing in November where we got some potentially promising signs with regard to intellectual property rights. It appears that China's leaders are willing now to com-

22

mit to a very high-level leadership structure, to be run by a vice premier, to really enforce against intellectual property theft.

We have made very strong statements to them about the importance of doing that, and obviously, as we say, the proof of the pudding is in the eating. So we are going to have to see what it is that they do, and we're going to be watching them very closely. We keep pushing, I promise you that.

Representative KAPTUR. Representative Reade, could I just ask you, in the automotive sector, if I look at our trade deficits with Asian nations, our trade competitors, I think today, even in Japan, less than 6 percent of the market is comprised of cars from anyplace in the world. They didn't even take Yugos.

A lot of their manufacturing is done, back-doored into China. We look at Korea, now we look at China. These translate into real job losses in our country. What can we do with the specific example that I referenced regarding Jeep Cherokees? What can the USTR do to get a level playing field for our automotive industry? What structures, what initiatives do you have set up to effectively deal with real, two-way market access?

Ms. READE. On automobiles, there was a very important WTO case on auto parts where there were discriminatory tariffs that created an unlevel playing field for our auto parts exporters. Work was done at the WTO to create an enforcement mechanism and China removed those problematic restrictions. So, there are some tools.

With regard to the issue of tariffs, that is what the Doha Round is focused on, trying to remove tariffs. That's another tool at our disposal. The other points that you're making though are, of course, incredibly important and we need to work very hard on trying to see what we can do at all times for such competitive industries and competitive U.S. exports, and that is our job and that's what we are trying hard to do. We welcome the opportunity to work with you on that.

Representative KAPTUR. You know, tariffs aren't the only means that keep products in or out. There are a lot of regulatory barriers and so forth. If we used Japan as a model of where we've not been able to gain access, what makes us think that our structures are effective relative to what will happen with China, or Korea? Why can't we get market access for the automotive industry? What's the problem?

Ms. READE. I am going to tell you very frankly that I am not an automotive industry expert. I am someone who knows China. I will be happy to take those notes down and try to see if I can get someone to give you a good and helpful response.

Representative KAPTUR. Mr. Chairman, I don't want to go over my time here. I really want to pursue this, because I've been around this place long enough to know that when the first President George Bush was President, the father, we had to create a special task force within USTR to try to brief up our negotiators because they knew nothing about the automotive industry. We had to send automotive executives to Tokyo to negotiate there.

You might recall, the first President Bush became ill. He was jet-lagged from the trip. We had auto executives sitting outside the room. To this day, this government has not been serious about market access in any of those Asian Tigers. It seems to me that something is very wrong. We have problems across the Pacific. We have got problems here. We are not organized. We are not organized to win or to get a—I appreciate your candor.

I think one of the major responsibilities USTR has is to take a look at the trade deficit numbers themselves and to look at just Japan, China, and Korea and ask yourself, which cars are on the roads there from anywhere else in the world? Really think hard about what we can do to open up market access for competitive products. We're not asking for the world here, just a fair playing field. But in the automotive sector we almost seem like we are defanged, like we don't either know what we're doing or we don't have the will to change this equation. The collateral damage is all over our country, and it's significant, very significant.

So this trade issue, Mr. Chairman—I thank you so much for addressing it in your testimony as well, and I thank Representative Reade for being here. But I would appreciate a very formal response from the administration on what we are going to do to redress these severe trade imbalances.

I would look at the automotive sector as an example of, we're not doing it right. It won't be any better in solar and it won't be any better in other fields. There is some trade, obviously, in agriculture. But if one looks at the deficits, they're staggering. It's harmed this country.

I sort of thought to myself that what this actually is, it's an old theory, maybe, after World War II when we viewed ourselves as a country in a certain way and that we thought that through some type of economic set of relationships we could move countries along.

But what has actually happened is that some of our fundamental political values have been compromised because we have basically given away the store and we haven't gotten more liberty for it in so many places around the world, including China. So I just wanted to implore you to please look at the automotive sector, look at it as one that you are to put your arms around. Look at Japan, look at Korea, and look at China and ask yourself, what is wrong with this equation? Thank you.

Thank you, Mr. Chairman.

Chairman SMITH. Thank you very much.

Just one final question. In our petition we noted that Section 301(d) of the Trade Act provides that a trading partner's persistent denial of workers' internationally recognized rights constitutes an unreasonable trade practice.

Section 301(b) authorizes the USTR and the President to take all appropriate and feasible actions to end China's repression of workers' rights if that repression burdens or restricts United States commerce. The Chinese Government's repression of workers' rights burdens the U.S. commerce by lowering the costs of China-based production and displacing millions of United States' workers. Do you believe that to be an accurate statement?

Ms. READE. I believe that you are flagging a very important issue and that it's one that has to be looked at.

Chairman SMITH. Could you get back as quickly as possible, for the record, on that too, if you would? This is ongoing and the workers are being exploited as we meet.

One final question. Your response to this, if this statement in your view is generally true or false. When migrants enter the factory system they often step into a nightmare of 12-hour to 18-hour work days, with no day of rest, earning minimum wages that may be withheld or unpaid altogether.

The factories are often sweltering, dusty, and damp. Workers are widely exposed to chemical toxins and hazardous machines, and suffer sicknesses, disfiguration, and death at the highest rates in world history. Some multinationals operating in China, under pressure from labor and consumer activists, have showcased factories that are well-lit and ventilated, but the vast majority of foreign-invested enterprises in China, as well as domestically owned enterprises, have no safety or health controls whatsoever. Is that accurate or inaccurate?

Ms. READE. You obviously have some detailed information on that subject and I would welcome seeing your source material. I think you are raising very critical issues here that our administration takes very seriously.

Chairman SMITH. Okay. I do raise this because these were in our petition that we filed on June 8, 2006. I know you were there. I'm not sure if you were privy to this information. Okay. But some people were and it seems to me that this information not only continues, in my opinion, to be accurate, it has probably gotten worse. So we'll get back to you on more of this in the future. So, I thank you.

I want to thank Ms. Reade for your testimony and for questions, and we look forward to your written responses. I would like to now welcome panel number two, beginning with Grant Aldonas, who is the principal managing director of Split Rock International, a Washington, DC based consulting and advisory firm he founded in 2006.

He was, from 2001 to 2005, the U.S. Under Secretary of Commerce for International Trade. Before assuming his position as Under Secretary of Commerce, Mr. Aldonas served as Chief International Trade Counsel to the Senate Finance Committee. He was a partner with Miller & Chevalier, a Washington, DC, law firm, prior to joining the Finance Committee.

We then will hear from Alan Price, partner and chair of the International Trade Practice of Wiley Rein. Mr. Price has more than 25 years of experience representing clients in high-profile, complex, international trade regulatory matters, including trade litigation involving public and government relations issues.

In addition to being chair of the firm's international trade practice, he heads the firm's antidumping and countervailing duty practice. He counsels clients on bilateral and multilateral agreements, trade legislation, Customs regulation, the Foreign Corrupt Practices Act, compliance issues, and Section 301 cases.

We will then hear from Clyde Prestowitz, who is founder and president of the Economic Strategy Institute [ESI]. Prior to founding ESI, he served as counsel to the Secretary of Commerce in the Reagan administration, where he led many U.S. trade or investment negotiations with Japan, China, Latin America, and Europe.

Before joining the Commerce Department he was a senior businessman in the United States, Europe, Japan, and throughout Asia and Latin America. He has served as vice chairman of the President's Committee on Trade and Investment in the Pacific, and sits on the Intel Policy Advisory Board and the U.S. Export-Import Bank Advisory.

Finally, we'll hear from Mr. Wei Jingsheng, who is a Chinese human rights and democracy advocate who was sentenced to jail twice, for a total of more than 18 years, due to his democratization activities, including an essay he wrote in 1978 entitled, "The Fifth Modernization: Democracy." For more than a decade since his exile he has published numerous articles and interviews about human rights and democracy in China, as well as international relations, economics, and trade.

Wei has received human rights and democracy awards, including the Robert F. Kennedy Memorial Human Rights Award, the European Parliament's Sakharov Prize for Freedom of Thought, and the National Endowment for Democracy's Award. He has been the chair of Overseas Chinese Democracy Coalition, OCDC, since 1998, president of Wei Jingsheng Foundation since 1998 as well, and president of the Asia Democracy Alliance, 2006.

Grant, if you could begin.

STATEMENT OF GRANT D. ALDONAS, PRINCIPAL MANAGING DIRECTOR, SPLIT ROCK INTERNATIONAL; FORMER UNDER SECRETARY OF COMMERCE FOR INTERNATIONAL TRADE (2001–2005)

Mr. ALDONAS. Thank you, Mr. Chairman, Congresswoman Kaptur. If I could, I'd like to submit my written statement for the record and simply summarize. I'll be very brief.

Chairman SMITH. Without objection, so ordered. Thank you.

Mr. ALDONAS. First, I want to say thanks. After having served on this Commission and having been a part of its creation actually when I was working on the Senate Finance Committee, I have enormous respect for the work and want to underscore the importance of what the Commission is doing.

Ten years ago when I appeared as a witness as Under Secretary of Commerce before the Commission, I made the point—two points, really. The first was that China's compliance with its WTO obligations was obviously the single most important factor in governing our bilateral trade relationship, and that we needed to see early, transparent, and measurable progress on compliance to satisfy ourselves that the deal we cut as a part of accession to the WTO, as well as the grant of permanent normal trade relationships, had served our interests.

The second point I made, which I believed at the time and I think events over the years have underscored that for me is the more important of the two, is the link between WTO compliance and the development of the rule of law in China.

I still think it's the more important measure, whether China's access to the WTO served our interests as well as that of the trading system, and I would suggest that China's future progress heavily depends on the extent to which it fosters a broader respect for the rule of law within China, a far lesser role for the state and the Communist Party, in the operation of the Chinese economy, and a steady erosion of the system of *guanxi,* the connections that dominate China's politics and its commerce. That, to me, is the acid test. I think you are focused on exactly the right issue.

One thing I was concerned about at the time, and remain concerned about, is that most explanations of China's rise, even in China, tend to ignore the extent to which its opening and its success have actually paralleled respect for the rule of law, starting with the special economic zones, then moving into the rest of China. What I mean when I say that it's not necessarily human rights alone that matter, but property rights, enforcement of contracts, things of that nature.

There is an underlying tension between the respect for the rule of law and the system of *guanxi*, or personal connections, that's formed a central institution of Chinese society since the days of Confucius. *Guanxi* is not necessarily a bad thing. In its most positive form it parallels much of Confucian thought with its heavy emphasis on reciprocal obligations in society, *ren,* and in that sense *guanxi,* can be taken to strengthen social cohesion.

But, unfortunately, what it also does, as is oftentimes the case, is foster corruption, nepotism, and in the process undermines or obstructs the development of rule of law and not reinforce the development of the rule of law. In that sense, *Guanxi* practice in China—and I think that's still true today, maybe more so—can yield the opposite of *ren* in terms of Confucian thought.

Relative to a system without laws, one can understand *guanxi* working efficiently as an economic matter, but the reverse isn't true. Sound laws with adequate processes for enforcement actually trump any system of *guanxi,* or personal connections, as a model of economic development. That is why I think China's future progress is linked directly to the extent to which it does choose to foster the rule of law. Unfortunately, there are a number of recent shifts that suggest China is not moving in that direction.

First, properly understood, policies like indigenous innovation undercut property rights and the sanctity of contracts, to which China owes much of its economic rise. Second, there is a generational shift underway in China which will bring to power a generation of princelings that benefit from, and foster, the system of *guanxi*. In my view, they are unlikely to embrace the rule of law precisely because it undercuts the power they otherwise wield within China's political system.

That leads me to a contradictory conclusion with respect to the central question before the Commission. The question was whether China's access to the WTO contributed to the development of the rule of law, and the answer in one sense is an unqualified yes. They obviously did change 2,000 laws at the national level, another 190,000 at the State and local levels.

Early on in the process there was a very strong effort, including the creation of institutions like the Shanghai WTO Center, which were models for trying to encourage compliance that reached beyond the ostensible changes in the amendments.

The problem is, that process began to degrade relatively quickly. In my own experience as Under Secretary of Commerce, it slowed down measurably. What had been a relatively open discussion and interest in implementing the WTO became a protracted negotiation that had to be driven toward an action-forcing event, like the meeting of the Joint Commission on Commerce and Trade, to produce any kind of progress at all.

Of course that led to the frustration that I think that then-USTR and now Senator Portman found when he was at USTR and launched the top-to-bottom review of our trade policy toward China, which I think reinforces many of the conclusions that both of you have made today, as well as the conclusions I'm stating here.

So in one sense it did contribute to the rule of law, but whether that proved sufficient to fundamentally change a political dynamic in China and resolve this contest in one sense between *guanxi* and connections and rule of law is a different question. The answer to that is no.

While I think the WTO rules have influenced China positively in terms of its legal development, I doubt whether they have the strength or the roots in Chinese society that, after only 10 years of somewhat halting implementation and observance, could offset this more powerful political shift that is currently under way in China.

So when I appeared before the Commission 10 years ago, I made the point that observance of the law in any society must become habit. It has to be woven into the fabric of social relationships. Unfortunately, that does not describe China today. It is hard, moreover, to see how the observance of the law becomes a deeply ingrained habit throughout Chinese society if the political leadership of the country doesn't practice it as well.

Let me stop there. I'd be happy to answer any questions you have. Thanks.

Chairman SMITH. Thank you so very much, Mr. Secretary.

Mr. Price?

[The prepared statement of Mr. Aldonas appears in the appendix.]

STATEMENT OF ALAN H. PRICE, PARTNER AND CHAIR, THE INTERNATIONAL TRADE PRACTICE, WILEY REIN, LLP

Mr. PRICE. Good afternoon, Chairman Smith, Chairman Brown, and Congresswoman Kaptur. I am Alan Price, head of the International Trade Practice at Wiley Rein. My testimony this afternoon represents my own personal views and is not offered on behalf of any client.

In the 10 years since it acceded to the WTO, China has systematically engaged in a pattern of avoiding, delaying, and directly violating its WTO commitments. In fact, China is increasingly manipulating the WTO system, exploiting loopholes, and working around existing rules in violation of the spirit, if not the letter, of the WTO agreements. This behavior is adversely impacting the United States and global economies, and undermines the legitimacy of the international rules-based trading system.

I have submitted lengthy written testimony for the record. I would like to focus my oral testimony on just three of the many areas where China has failed to comply with its WTO commitments.

First, the Chinese Government continues to exercise significant government ownership and control over key segments of its economy and to heavily intervene in the commercial decisions of its state-owned enterprises [SOEs].

This behavior is contrary to its WTO commitments to refrain from influencing the decisions of its SOEs and to require SOEs to operate based solely on commercial considerations. Moreover, I would add that to support its SOEs the Chinese Government continues to grant massive subsidies to these enterprises, as I have detailed, in the steel industry and in other industries.

A second major area of Chinese WTO non-compliance is its imposition of market-distorting export restrictions. In clear violation of its WTO commitments, China imposes export quotas, export taxes, discretionary export licensing regimes, minimum export prices, and other measures designed to limit its exports of raw materials.

In fact, in July 2011, a WTO dispute settlement panel found that China's maintenance of its export restrictions on various raw materials was inconsistent with its WTO obligations and recommended that China come into compliance with its commitments.

Despite this ruling, China continues to impose WTO-inconsistent export restrictions on a variety of raw materials, including the so-called rare earths. These measures are designed to keep raw materials in China and to advantage Chinese-consuming industries at the expense of consuming industries in the United States and around the globe.

Third, China continues to manipulate its currency, in violation of its WTO commitments. Specifically, consistent with WTO rulings, China's currency manipulation appears to be a prohibited export subsidy because it is designed to principally benefit China's exporters.

There can be little doubt that China's currency manipulation is the biggest subsidy of all. Currency is also actionable at the WTO because it nullifies and impairs the benefits accruing to the United States under GATT 1994, and because it frustrates the intent of the WTO agreements under GATT Article 15, Paragraph 4.

China's repeated failures to comply with its WTO obligations have come at great cost to the U.S. and global economies. Indeed, China's status as the world's second-largest economy makes its failure to live up to many of its WTO obligations all the more troubling.

Given its size and economic influence, China's refusal to abide by many of its WTO commitments not only harms the U.S. and third-country economic interests, but threatens to undermine the legitimacy of the WTO and the international rules-based trading system.

To address these failures, the United States must take a more proactive approach. First, the United States should aggressively litigate China's WTO violations. Second, Congressman Smith, I agree with you that the United States should stress reciprocity as a guiding principal for all trade and investment issues related to China. Third, the United States should build bipartisan and multilateral coalitions with trading partners to limit China's artificial advantages.

Fourth, the United States should press for a new, reconfigured round of WTO negotiations. The new round will be premised in large part on eliminating the loopholes in the existing system that

China has used to its advantage. In order to motivate China to agree to a new round, we will need to succeed in many of the afore-mentioned items.

In short, what is needed is a bold, concerted, and coordinated effort by Congress and the executive branch to send a clear signal to China that it must end its trade-distorting policies and practices. Thank you.

Chairman SMITH. Mr. Price, thank you very much. Your full statement will be made a part of the record, both the two witnesses'. Very incisive remarks, and I do thank you.

Now we'll go to Mr. Prestowitz. Is that right? Thank you.

[The prepared statement of Mr. Price appears in the appendix.]

STATEMENT OF CLYDE V. PRESTOWITZ, JR., FOUNDER AND PRESIDENT, ECONOMIC STRATEGY INSTITUTE

Mr. PRESTOWITZ. I guess that if you had heard 10 years ago, if the people testifying 10 years ago had come in and told you that 10 years down the road the United States would have a $250 billion trade deficit with China, that a couple of million jobs would have been off-shored from the United States to China, that the dynamics of the relationship would result in China holding a $3 trillion fund, effectively, solely under the control of the Chinese Communist Party, I guess that you would have been not terribly enthusiastic about the deal.

But you didn't hear that. Rather, what you heard from Charlene Barshefsky, the U.S. Trade Representative, was that China is not at all like Japan. You remember that in the 1980s and 1990s we had had very similar issues with Japan, and Ambassador Barshefsky assured the Congress that China is not at all like Japan. At that time there were estimates of 800,000 jobs possibly to be lost, and Ambassador Barshefsky said this was absurd.

You heard from the Institute on International Economics that the then-trade deficit of $68 billion was really incorrectly counted, it was only $43 billion, and again that China was totally different than Japan, and that estimates of a rising trade deficit with China were absurd.

You heard from the Brookings Institute the same thing. In other words, all of the think tanks in town, all of the officials that you talked to, with one or two exceptions, painted a rosy picture of rising U.S. exports, rising jobs, and a win-win. That was obviously wrong. Obviously everybody who came before you 10 years ago was profoundly wrong. Not everybody. A couple were correct, but not many.

What was wrong? Why were they so wrong? The reason they were so wrong is because they were then, and we still today—our policymakers today, still are operating on the basis of false premises. The premise of all of these discussions is that we and China and many other countries, of course, are members of the WTO and the IMF, and other regional and bilateral arrangements, and that we have all embraced the principles of free trade, according to Adam Smith and David Ricardo, and that we are all practicing these principles and that if there are problems it must be because somebody is cheating, and if we just enforce the rules then the whole thing will work properly.

This is very much influenced by the faith—I would almost say the religion of free trade fundamentalism—that has gripped Washington for most of the past 30 years, which insists that simplistic, comparative advantage and unilateral free trade is somehow going to be a win-win for all the parties.

It insists that, despite evidence mounting to the contrary. I could not help but think, as I was sitting and listening to the previous testimony, looking at Congresswoman Kaptur. Marcy, how many times have we heard this story? How many times have we heard the same comments? Yes, we're looking into it. Yes, give us the information. Japan, Korea, Taiwan, Singapore. We keep going through this and it's because if you keep banging your head against the wall and expecting a different result, you're crazy. Well, we're crazy.

So this brings me then to, what can we do? What I want to say is that the discussion here today about, is China in compliance with WTO, how can we enforce the rules, can the USTR be more aggressive, in a way I think it's beside the point.

I don't think that you can enforce the rules. For one reason, the rules are not that clear. Alan mentioned nullification and impairment, and I agree with him that there are provisions to deal with nullification and impairment. You can make an argument that some of the measures that China is engaging in are nullifying and impairing, but it's not at all clear that you could win that case actually in the WTO. So I don't think you can enforce the rules, number one.

Number two, I think that you won't enforce the rules, or let's say no administration will enforce the rules, because enforcing the rules means that there's going to be conflict with China. We have a lot of fish to fry with China. We want China to help us with North Korea, with Iran, on climate change, all kinds of issues which are going to lead an administration—any administration—to hesitate to get involved in really massive conflict over trade and economics.

Finally, even if you could and would enforce the rules, I don't think it'll make any difference because essentially what's going on here is a whole different approach to economic development. In the United States and in other parts of the globe, the notion of the market is, the market is an end in itself. If an outcome is a market-based outcome, it's accepted as legitimate. But in other parts of the world, in Germany, in Japan, in Korea, in China, the market is a tool to get you to an outcome.

The outcome is, we want to build a steel industry, we want to build a high-speed rail industry, we want to build an aircraft industry, we want to build a semiconductor industry. If the market gets us there, great. If it doesn't get us there, what kind of subsidies do we need? So you are dealing with an entirely different mentality and it's not going to conform to any set of rules that will inhibit that progress toward economic development.

So that leaves you, I think, only with the alternative that of course you can use the rules and use investigations as a way to stimulate negotiations, but really what the United States needs to do is to act more like China.

The United States needs to have the same emphasis on its own economic development and on countering the distortions in the market that come from currency manipulation, financial investment packages, and binational policies in a way that will foster investment and development and competitiveness in the United States.

Thank you.

Chairman SMITH. Thank you very much.

Wei Jingsheng?

STATEMENT OF WEI JINGSHENG, OVERSEAS CHINESE DEMOCRACY COALITION

Mr. WEI. Thank you to the Chairman and the Cochairman, and thank you to Representative Kaptur. Once the United States granted China PNTR status, China successfully joined the WTO shortly after. For the past decade, Chinese exports have grown substantially, leading to the rapid growth of its GDP.

However, two results come out of this growth. On the U.S. side, the trade deficit with China has rapidly increased, along with rapidly increasing unemployment and national debt. Meanwhile, on the Chinese side the total consumption by the Chinese people did not grow synchronously, nor did the imports from the United States.

From another view, in the past 10 years since China entered the WTO, gross United States manufacturing has been slow and China's consumption has grown slowly as well. A larger portion of the growth in both countries was exchanged into cash, which not only had an impact on the financial market, but also expanded the wealth gap between the rich and the poor in both countries. The normal development of these two giant economic entities is the root cause of the global economic recession in recent years.

Further, the deformed economic development originated in an unfair trade relationship. In other words, the United States and Europe opened their markets to China, while China did not open its market to either the United States or Europe. Meanwhile, the Chinese Government has been using unfair methods for competition, especially by way of under-valuing the Chinese currency.

Thus, China has been able to develop its manufacturing industry, while inhibiting the development of the United States' and Europe's manufacturing industry. At the same time, the Chinese consumer market was not expanded and its imports were not increased. The profit that was realized—from unfair trading mostly—fell into the pockets of multinational corporations and the Chinese Government.

When people talk about the wonderful slogan of free trade, they forget that free trade needs some basic conditions. The domestic economy in China is neither "free trade," nor a "free market." The Chinese Communist Government is always the biggest controller of the Chinese market.

Regardless of whether you are a foreign company or a Chinese company, you can only obtain market share or market access with the permission of the Chinese Government. The condition for this access and share is defined by the Chinese Government's need and international politics, as well as the control of imports of foreign

32

groups into China. The strategic purpose of this control is to keep most of the Chinese domestic market for Chinese enterprises, especially those state-owned, less-efficient businesses that lack world competition.

In the past 10 years, the Chinese Communist Government continues naked trade protection measures. As China is not a free country both politically and economically, so the government will not use nor is it used to carry out terms according to the World Trade Organization law, or as it promised.

Also, because Chinese law is not binding to the government—so there are a number of WTO conditions even though they were absorbed into Chinese law, they will not be enforced any more than the other laws. Chinese law is understood as tools for the officials, so they will be executed if they are considered favorably for officials and they will not be executed if they are not.

That is, the WTO simply cannot restrain China's economic behavior. It is impossible to eliminate all forms of trade barriers in China, including the Chinese Government's manipulation of the Chinese currency. It is impossible to make China a free trade country.

I will talk on this real quick, since our time is up. Basically, it's that the WTO laws will not be implemented by China, so therefore we must enforce it. So there are two possibilities for changing this massively unfair trading relationship. One, is to exclude China from the WTO. The other, is that you must do it on your own.

Finally, I hope that the U.S. Congress and the U.S. administration can fully understand that because of the special rules in the Chinese legal system, as well as the irregularity of the market caused by the Chinese authoritarian political system, we should not use a normal way of thinking in the normal society of the United States to understand the Chinese affairs, which are totally different.

[The prepared statement of Mr. Wei appears in the appendix.]

Chairman SMITH. Mr. Wei, thank you very much for your testimony.

Let me just go to a couple of questions, because the hour is late. But I do thank you all for very incisive remarks.

Secretary Aldonas, in your testimony you talked about the first case brought against China under WTO was during the Bush administration in 2004 with regard to semiconductor producers and the preferences that the Chinese market had or companies had. You said that China acted to preempt the need for a definitive ruling and implemented a plan to bring itself into compliance.

It raises the question about enforcement in general. How many cases have been brought? Are there other cases where, realizing that they were clearly in the wrong, they move quickly and deftly to avoid a ruling from WTO? And in part of that, how many of the companies are fearful of retaliation if they were to press for protection from an unfair trading practice?

Mr. ALDONAS. Yes, that's a great question. I'd like to say, in defense of the WTO and the agreement that was reached, it has in fact worked in terms of the dispute settlement process when the cases have been brought to the WTO. China has been willing to engage in that process. The Chinese have adhered to the results when the results have gone against them.

The 2004 case was an example that I cited for two reasons, Congressman. One was because it worked at the time, but what you began to see relatively quickly thereafter was the erosion of the willingness or the concern about seeing a ruling in an international body against China that would imply that it wasn't living up to its WTO obligations. We are well past that now. I don't think there's any embarrassment in China about indigenous innovation or any of the other policies that I would regard as potential violations of the WTO.

But to the extent that the process has been one where we have submitted claims, China has engaged in the process and has adhered to the outcome as a part of that. That's the better part of what's happened inside the WTO, relative to the impact that China has had on negotiations, for example.

To your second point, there are clearly instances where American companies have been unwilling to pursue not only what I thought were clear WTO violations, but more profoundly the theft of intellectual property by their own partners, because they were afraid of what the potential retaliation might be.

It comes in subtle forms. If you think of General Motors, at a time when it was making no money in the United States and the UAW was bargaining for raises from General Motors, those raises were paid for by sales of GM vehicles in China, where the best-selling automobile in China is a Buick. General Motors' willingness to take on potential trade problems in China was, in part, compromised by the practical need to keep selling in China. You can see the dynamic that creates for the American economy.

Now, my view of what Claire said, who's an old friend; we've known each other for 30 years. I know she's doing a great job at USTR, but one of the things that you have to do at that point as a member of the executive branch is be willing to go at the issue for the company. Right? Even without names.

Because the reality is, oftentimes when you're at the JCCT relative to a WTO dispute settlement process, you can find a way to solve practical problems and try and move some measure along. I wouldn't call it WTO compliance, but I would say that looking after our commercial interests is just as important in that context, and throwing a brush-back pitch against the Chinese is always useful.

The question is whether or not in those settings American officials are willing actually to take up their cudgels without having to force a company to name names, go public, or file a 301 petition. I think the administration is doing a better job of trying to solicit actionable cases and trying to move ahead, but not aggressively enough.

I liken it to what the Justice Department used to do with civil rights litigation. Even when they thought they might lose a case, they were very aggressive in pushing the point, even to the point of trying to make law as a part of it. Frankly, I'd like to see even more of that, and I think Claire is willing to do it at USTR. Many of the issues that China presents fall in the penumbra of the WTO obligations, and are not squarely violations. As Alan was pointing out, they can nonetheless result in nullification and impairment of our WTO rights.

Unless we're really willing to take on that set of issues and start to make law, one way or another, either to illuminate the problem in the trading system or in fact to get the enforcement we want, we actually haven't done our job on behalf of those American companies.

Chairman SMITH. Mr. Price, you mentioned that currency is actionable at WTO. Why hasn't that been brought? And you also went through a number of others: Government procurement, indigenous innovation, intellectual property rights, circumvention of U.S. trade orders, transparency issues. It seems as if we've been asleep at the switch. Your statement?

Mr. PRICE. There are a number of issues and problems out there. With regard to currency, I have been working on this issue for probably eight years now, and cutting across both administrations there has been an unwillingness to make the tough decisions.

It's very easy to say it's a Treasury obligation and it's very easy to try to negotiate, but unless there is some attempt to move the ball forward in a more forceful way, we are simply not making any progress. Eight years is a long time to not make progress. Whatever minimal changes have happened in the exchange rate over the last 18 months are just that, minimal.

I agree with Clyde that it is not clear that the current system can fully tackle this, but we haven't tried. We need to be more aggressive, we need to take these tough issues, and as Mr. Aldonas has said, we may win these, we may lose these, but we will not know unless we try. If we lose these, then we know what needs to be fundamentally changed in the system.

There is absolutely a need for more aggressive enforcement. It cuts through currency; it cuts through a number of these other issues that you have named. Without tackling these broader issues, we are going to continue to lose in this trade relationship.

Chairman SMITH. Let me ask you, in terms of personal financial gain, we've had a number of instances—and I was involved with a few related to my own district—where, as part of their foreign sourcing, they just looked at the bottom line of labor costs and then uprooted and moved to China.

In one case they actually moved to Mexico. It was the American Standard, where the toilets are made. It was in my district, and it's now in Mexico because they could pay much less to the workers. That CEO, by the way—one of the CEOs I'm talking about actually got a big raise right after.

I mean, how much of this is just pure short-term gain for certain higher echelon people in business, very often who are the big donors and bundlers for political campaigns, particularly at the White House level, who then end up like GE is, moving all their health, technology manufacturing to China. It seems to me it's just a myopic, short-term view there. Some people get very rich in the short term.

Second, why isn't the USTR and Department of Defense more concerned about dual-use items, especially since the conditions that China puts on market access and the transfer of intellectual property? The Global Online Freedom bill that I have is focusing, too, on export controls of surveillance equipment and the like that's not just used by the secret police to hunt down people like Wei Jingsheng, but also has dual applicability for their military, which now is growing exponentially, Blue Water navy, and all that. Why don't we get that?

It seems to me that part of that short-mindedness or short focus doesn't understand how the government so effectively uses even the opium wars, the two opium wars, as a way of continually harping against the west—England in that case more than anyone else. But it just seems like we didn't get that. We misperceive the animosity there on the government level. The people, I think, unfortunately are subjected to that. If you could, whoever would like.

Mr. ALDONAS. Just to pick up your point on the export control side, I was actually thinking while you were talking earlier that the conditions you want to impose on the surveillance equipment that my first job back in the Department of State when I was a young Foreign Service officer was in an office called the Office of East-West Trade, which thankfully no longer exists. It died with the Cold War.

But at the time, one of the things I had to do was approve the applications for exports to China of things like Texas Instruments 99As. The reality is, a lot of the things that we sent in the way of ICT technology exported have contributed to greater openness in China. No doubt about it, right?

But we do have to be very concerned about the aspects of those technologies that can be used by the Chinese Government to reinforce their control. If you recall, under apartheid we controlled equipment like this to South Africa because we didn't want to support the idea that the South African police could snoop on their own people. I don't see that as different in China.

So if you really want the value of the technology to work in favor of freedom and the rights that we value in our society, the kind of bill you're talking about makes a lot of sense. The idea that you don't have the State Department and the Commerce Department, which are much more concerned with the dual-use items than the Defense Department, thinking along those lines when our paramount goal should be to foster the freedom that being online encourages. There is even a commercial reason for encouraging freedom on the Internet in China. The reality is, that for our firms to export, they have to overcome high search costs in China. In the absence of having this conduit protected so that you can participate in the market through that venue openly, it's very difficult to enter any market around the world.

So the irony is, the bill that you're talking about would serve our commercial interests, as well as saying in a demonstrable way that we're not accepting of what these tools could be used for, whether it's to head somebody to the laogai or whether it is something more nefarious in terms of industrial secrets.

Mr. WEI. I have been a long-time supporter of the Online Freedom Act proposed by Representative Smith. I want to say one thing, that the companies have to lobby with the Chinese Government. So this bill is something the Chinese Government dislikes most, so it will be also the hardest to go through the U.S. Congress.

We don't have the evidence to say directly, but indeed when we were advocating Internet freedom to supporters, Representative Smith's proposal, those aides and staff of some congressional Members say that they received tremendous pressure against it.

So I want to say for the last 10 years since China entered the WTO, not only has the United States lost a lot of money economically, but they also lost quite a bit politically because you could see the control of the Chinese Government over the American politics.

Chairman SMITH. Thank you.

Mr. PRESTOWITZ. I just wanted to add one point.

Chairman SMITH. Yes.

Mr. PRESTOWITZ. Which is, you made the point about U.S. companies or executives making short-term decisions to move production, and maybe they get immediately a lower cost, but there's some long-term price. I think this is part of the problem. You have to put yourself in the position of, let's say the CEO of Intel or GE [General Electric], global companies. You have to remember that these companies are incorporated in America, but they're not really American companies.

A company like GE has more employees outside the United States than it has in the United States. Its shareholders are global. Jeff Immelt, chairman of GE, has constituencies, political constituencies, investment constituencies all over the world. So even if he wanted to, he can't really make decisions that somehow, out of some patriotic fervor, are special for the United States. He's got to treat his employees kind of equally.

Second, he operates in a world in which the incentives in the global economy are pretty much to move the production of tradeable goods and the provision of tradeable services out of the United States. What are those incentives? The incentives are that the dollar is over-valued and it's kept over-valued by the intervention or the manipulation policies not just of China. A number of other countries are manipulating their currency also.

Second, many countries provide very aggressive investment incentives. Intel recently put a Pentium chip plant in China. Pentium chips cannot be produced on an operating cost lower in China than in the United States. The United States is the low-cost, high-quality place to make Pentium chips.

Why is the plant going to China? A number of reasons, but a big reason is that of the $5 or $7 billion investment, the Chinese Government is putting up a couple billion dollars. So that makes a big difference. We don't match that. The United States has no match to those kinds of investment incentives.

A third incentive is that every time an executive goes to China and meets with Hu Jintao or Wen Jiabao or the janitor on the floor, all that executive hears is, "When are you going to put a factory in China? When are you going to put technology and research and development in China?"

Now, there's a little threat in that question because we know China is not a society of rule of law. So the unspoken subtle undertone here is, if you don't put a factory here, who knows what might happen? The electricity is what Mr. Ray has been talking about, the informal power of a bureaucracy that is not transparent and has great discretionary authority. So they're scared.

Now, in that kind of an environment, to ask a U.S. CEO to invest in the United States because he's American and that's the patriotic thing to do, this is fantasy. You've got to change the incentives. So you've got to change that incentive structure and that means you've got to deal with the currency issue, and the investment issue, and the pressure issue, and the binational issue, and some others.

And while I am fully supportive of Alan and Grant in enforcing the rules, and let's be aggressive in enforcing the rules, to really change those incentives is going to require a lot more than just filing cases in the WTO or filing antidumping or countervailing duty cases in the United States.

Chairman SMITH. Just to follow up on that, when you talk about treating employees equally, and that there are constituent parts to an Intel and the like, the problem is that the laborers in China are not treated equally and that's why I asked the USTR, and will ask again, that they initiate an investigation pursuant to 301, that there's an unfair trading practice because of the massive exploitation of the individual, especially migrant folks.

So I'm for free and fair trade, but not when it's unfair because of—I mean, our workers can't compete with that. So the CEO may be listening to other members of the board, but at some point you say, "Hey, do we go in there and cruelly treat these people?" And they are treated——

Mr. PRESTOWITZ. Well, I'm with you. But honestly, I don't believe that Jeff Immelt is consciously making decisions to mistreat Chinese workers.

Chairman SMITH. No. But is he aware? I mean, that's the issue.

Mr. PRESTOWITZ. Yes, I think he is.

Chairman SMITH. How aware is he? No, no.

Mr. PRESTOWITZ. Look, for example, if you said Wal-Mart, I think because they're out-sourcing a lot of the production through other companies, I'm not sure whether Wal-Mart would know what's happening. But in the case of a company like Intel or GE, I think they're pretty aware and I think they do treat their people pretty well, wherever they are.

Chairman SMITH. Let me just say very briefly that right before President Clinton capitulated on linking most-favored-nation status with human rights, which he did the year before with great fanfare, and myself and so many others took to the floor and thanked him profusely, only to say that it is an insincere commitment to human rights.

As you know, he de-linked on May 26, 1994, late on a Friday afternoon when nobody was watching. Everybody was out of town here, and it was like the big non-issue. As Wei has said, and Harry Wu has said, and so many others, that threw the dissidents right under the bus and they've never reclaimed it since.

The issue of exploitation of labor has been a problem with successive administrations and nobody has addressed it. So just to look back, and I mentioned this but I will be very quick on this, every CEO should read the Cox Commission, where Loral and Hughes gave away or sold, and then lavishly funded, the presidential candidate that enabled all that, Bernie Schwartz and others. That was outrageous, in my opinion, for such a short-term, big payday for those two companies. But to give away satellite technology that is second to none—we know now that our satellites are in grave danger of some of those technologies—yes, Mr. Secretary?

Mr. ALDONAS. I want to go back to the labor point. You know, one thing that's always struck me is the way the trade and labor argument is postulated. It may be worth, particularly in the context of the discussion about China, to think about it the way it should be thought about. If you think about what free trade is designed to do, it's really designed to create the opportunities for specialization that allow you to raise your productivity.

The irony is, in a system without sound labor rules that actually allow you to bargain freely for the full value of your labor, there's no incentive to take advantage of that opportunity for specialization. So if what you're saying is free trade, at least in my view, what you are talking about is also a system where the labor market is open and contestable, along with everything else.

If you have a system, the *danwei*—that is, work units—and all the other things that are a part of the Chinese system of labor control over time—which remain strong in the countryside, although not necessarily in urban areas—the reality is you don't have a system that actually provides the advantage of free trade or WTO accession to the Chinese worker, and in the process you're denying a similar set of rights to an American worker as a part of the process.

So the irony is, and in part it's because of the way our unions have argued the trade and labor issue, we have failed to think constructively about how trade and labor rights relate. Organized labor wants a tool inside the context of a trade agreement to be able to rap somebody on the knuckles and, oftentimes, to look for protection.

But, there is a substantive reason why you would want labor rules to be discussed in the context of trade, and it leads to a broader point which I really think is where Clyde has been going. To be honest, what the last 10 years has demonstrated is there is a risk in negotiating simply about trade barriers, countervailing duties, government procurement, when in fact two countries have very different premises for the basis of organizing their economy and organizing production.

What that suggests is, when you sit down to a negotiation you should be thinking very hard about making sure that you've either got the premises right or you've got the tools to offset the unfair advantages that may stem from those differences. Right now, to be honest with you we have an opportunity, if the President decides to use it, in the Trans-Pacific Partnership [TPP].

President Obama describes the TPP as a 21st century trade agreement, which is literally true because we're in the 21st century and he's negotiating it. But, if what President Obama pressed for was more than a conventional trade agreement—one that required open and contestable markets across all factors of production, including labor, as a part of the process in this regional arrangement, what you may find, since I don't believe China will be pushed, is that the Chinese nonetheless may find that the incentive created by those rules for investment in Vietnam, investment in the United

States, investment in other partners, makes them more competitive than China.

It may finally create an incentive where the Chinese have to start moving in the same direction—i.e., toward the rule of law— of their own volition because they'll start to see that their "Go-West" strategy of encouraging investment beyond the Chinese coastline won't work, that Vietnam becomes the new south coast of China, and that this churn that allows people to come out of the hinterlands and to the coast for work starts to break down as an economic model for China.

So in one sense we have a tool that's positive trade-wise to try and address this problem, but it requires a very different concept along the lines Clyde is talking about—a very different approach— to how you sit down and bargain about the rules in a trade agreement. What I would suggest is that, in a world in which we compete in a globalized economy, we will have fundamentally missed the direction that our trade policy has to go if we fail to adopt that approach.

Chairman SMITH. Just two final questions. The new round of negotiations. Is it a pipe dream at WTO or is it something that might happen? Whether or not Xi Jinping, who follows Hu Jintao—will he have any different take on human rights, rule of law, and trade?

And finally, so three, Mr. Price, you mentioned that China has engaged in a consistent pattern of avoiding, delaying, and directly violating its WTO commitments. Yet if you turn on CNBC Tonight, they talk about China having the imprimatur of WTO. It just kind of puts a veneer and a protection over how well or poorly or not at all that China has lived up to its obligations.

China has on so many international agreements—the International Covenant for Civil and Political Rights—they sign it, they talk about it as if they're following it, and they don't. I'm wondering, it seems like the best-kept secret on Wall Street, and maybe even in Washington, is that China has failed miserably to live up to its commitments on WTO. So, you might want to take a stab at that. Why does it remain such a secret?

Mr. PRESTOWITZ. Well, on that last point——

Chairman SMITH. Yes, please.

Mr. PRESTOWITZ [continuing]. Wall Street, and many of the global companies are benefiting from that. I mean, the under-valuation of the Chinese currency is very beneficial to a lot of U.S. and other global companies who are operating in China. So they don't particularly object. In fact, they will lobby here against any response to the currency issue, so I think that's a very important reason why a lot of this doesn't go forward.

The second reason it doesn't come forward is the one you mentioned earlier, which is that there is fear. They can be retaliated against. They don't like to be too public. You heard in the earlier testimony from Ms. Reade, companies don't necessarily volunteer to come in to see the USTR and talk about problems because then they become visible and they can be attacked.

Mr. PRICE. I think Clyde has hit on a couple of the key issues. Clearly, there is a separation between our national economic interests and the discrete interests of individual companies there. Many companies are invested, and therefore compromising their ability to support a message here.

In terms of how you get from where we are today to where we need to go, that is the difficult issue. That is really the hard question here. China is part of a club. We invited them into the clubhouse at this point. Essentially, it is impossible to force them out of the clubhouse unless they want to voluntarily withdraw from the WTO or we would voluntarily withdraw from the WTO, neither of which at this point seems terribly likely. Or you have to develop pressure points. You have to forcefully have a message.

It has to be led by the administration and Congress. You have to look at your pressure points, emphasize reciprocity where you can so that you fight starting the game. Even if we may be in technical violation on some of the rules in the same way that they are, you have to be willing to aggressively litigate at the WTO, point out these fundamental flaws, and try to solve the problems. It may be that not every attempt works, but in totality if we are going to try to solve these problems we have to aggressively tackle them, and tackle them quickly.

Next, the potential of getting to a new round that could work. The current formulation of the Doha Round does not work. With all due respect to the administration witness, it is widely acknowledged that the Doha Round has essentially failed at this point. It almost prevents realistic negotiations by trying to continue within that framework, but we have to take a number of steps to get to the point where we could get a new framework, where we can get enough international consensus to force China to the table. TPP is part of that. There are a variety of steps there but it is going to take a while and going to take fairly aggressive and concerted action to get there.

Mr. ALDONAS. I'd say, Mr. Chairman, it won't happen in the WTO. The reality is, Doha is dead. It has been dead for a longtime. The only question is how we're going to give it a decent burial.

In terms of starting new negotiations, the logic is the same, China being the example today, but India is a problem. There are a variety of others. But if you think about China, China basically said, we paid at the office in our accession process. We're unwilling to engage in further liberalization.

Under those circumstances, which are deeply inconsistent with the idea of launching a new round of negotiations and not bearing your part of the burden of contributing to the ongoing process in the WTO, the reality is that hasn't changed. In fact, it's going in the wrong direction.

So, the idea that the system within the WTO where the individual players within the WTO are going to come to a different conclusionabout what they should be bargaining for, I really doubt. That's why I think all the pressure, not just in the United States'context but in all other contexts, is really moving toward bilateral and regional agreements.

A second point is about Wall Street's impact on industrial organization. A lot of what I do in my business is work with companies and their global supply chains. You would be amazed at what Wall Street analysts say to companies.The pressure there is, why aren't you out-sourcing? There's a mantra, in effect, an assumption that out-sourcing is the answer tocutting your costs.

As Clyde points out, there are plenty of industries, Intel being one of them, where the labor costs are minuscule in terms of whatthey produce relative to the value of the product, and so it can't be wages. Out-sourcing isn't necessarily the right strategy.Yet, the pressure from Wall Street analysts on your stock is to say, how come you don't have a plan for out-sourcing? Ironically,whatever Dodd-Frank did, it certainly didn't change any of the pressure the companies that I deal with feel from Wall Street when they're thinking about sourcing.

I do agree with Clyde that we have to get back to that level of thinking about the incentives in our system and what we're tryingto produce. Do we want an innovative economy with broadly shared prosperity or do we want one that's essentially a winner-take-all system?

A last point about Hu's replacement. It's very hard to see how, given the other shift in terms of the generation that's comingon-stream, that his replacement could be like Zedillo in Mexico, in essence, rejecting the Party structure from which he sprang. Even though Hu's replacement saw his father sent to the hinterland during the Cultural Revolution, as did Bo Xilai and a number of the other princelings, the reality is, there is too much to ask of that one individual to run against the grain of his entire generation to say they're going to make that choice.

To the extent change comes, it's going to have to come from the bottom because the Chinese people, like Mr. Wei, demand it.That is why many of the things you talk about trying to open up the vehicles for that type of protest to take place and whyyou need strong advocacy from the United States about the values we cherish and we want to see implemented around the world andshouldn't be shy about it.

Chairman SMITH. Mr. Wei?

Mr. WEI. For the Chinese Government, it got great benefits from this one-way trade, so, of course, the Chinese Government would not want to give up this benefit. However, the question is why the American Government would let this kind of bleeding go on as it is.

American big business has made lots of money, and then the politicians are influenced by those big businesses. I think that's the fundamental reason why the American Government is so weak on the China issue. Although some American businesses made money, the American people lost their jobs.

The American economy is in terrible shape. So I really think that this is the time that the American people and American politicians really need to have more participation. To those people who do not follow the law or rule—you must have a really hardliner standard, including the upcoming Communist leader, Xi Jinping.

According to my personal source, I know that Xi Jinping may be more open-minded, maybe a little newer than the old Chinese Communist leaders. However, if there is no strong stand or push by the U.S. Government, I am afraid that he's not going to take that stand either. So my conclusion is, the American Government must be very hard-lined and very strong. I agree with what the friends next to me have said. Thank you.

Chairman SMITH. Thank you.

Anything else before we conclude?

[No response].

Chairman SMITH. Without objection, I ask that a statement by Senator Levin be made a part of the record.

Again, I want to thank our very distinguished witnesses for your very wise counsel and recommendations and analysis of the problem.

The hearing is adjourned.

[The prepared statement of Senator Levin appears in the appendix.]

[Whereupon, at 5:06 p.m. the hearing was adjourned.]

APPENDIX

Prepared Statements

Prepared Statement of Claire E. Reade

December 13, 2011

Introduction

Chairman Smith, Chairman Brown and members of the Commission, I appreciate the opportunity to testify today on issues surrounding the U.S.-China trade relationship and, in particular, China's efforts to fulfill the commitments that it made upon joining the World Trade Organization (WTO) ten years ago. This is a subject of considerable importance and a matter of great priority for the Administration and the U.S. Trade Representative (USTR) Ron Kirk.

I would like to begin my testimony with USTR's assessment of China's first ten years of WTO membership, followed by a discussion of some specific areas of ongoing concern. I will then address the impact of China's WTO membership on the rule of law in China, with an emphasis on the issue of transparency. Finally, I will share my observations about what China's future participation in the WTO might look like.

Overall Assessment of China's WTO Compliance

When China acceded to the World Trade Organization on December 11, 2001, the terms of its accession called for China to implement numerous specific commitments over time, with almost all of its commitments to be phased in completely within five years. Following China's accession, Chinese leaders took many impressive steps to implement a set of sweeping reforms in order to meet these commitments. China reduced tariffs, eliminated many non-tariff barriers that denied national treatment and market access for goods and services imported from other WTO members, and made legal improvements in intellectual property protections and in transparency. These steps unquestionably deepened China's integration into the international trading system, strengthening both China's rule of law and the economic reforms that China had begun in 1978. Trade and investment also expanded dramatically between China and its many trading partners, including the United States. Indeed, this expansion in trade and investment has provided numerous and substantial opportunities for U.S. businesses, workers, farmers and service suppliers, and a wealth of affordable goods for U.S. consumers.

Despite this progress, the overall picture of China's actions to implement its WTO policy commitments remains complex, given a troubling trend in China toward intensified state intervention in the Chinese economy over the last five years. Increasingly, trade frictions with China can be traced to China's pursuit of industrial policies that rely on trade-distorting government actions to promote or protect China's state-owned enterprises and domestic industries. In fact, in recent years, China seems to be embracing state capitalism more strongly, rather than continuing to move toward the economic reform goals that originally drove its pursuit of WTO membership.

Specific Areas of Concern

In short, even with the tremendous progress China has made in the complex task of implementing its WTO commitments, critical work remains. Today, I will highlight four areas that continue to cause particular concern for the United States and U.S. stakeholders in terms of China's approach to the obligations of WTO membership. For more details about these matters, I would refer the Commission to the 2011 USTR Report to Congress on China's WTO Compliance, which we issued yesterday. I will submit a copy for the record.

The first area is effective enforcement of intellectual property rights in China. This remains a massive challenge. Counterfeiting and piracy in particular remain at unacceptably high levels in China and continue to cause serious harm to U.S. businesses across many sectors of the economy. Trade secret theft is also becoming very worrisome.

Second, China's pursuit of an array of industrial policies raises serious concerns. Examples of these policies include excessive subsidies, discriminatory policies aimed at promoting "indigenous innovation," export restraints on raw materials, the pursuit of unique national standards, and restrictions on foreign investment. These policies benefit state-owned enterprises, as well as other favored companies attempting to move up the economic value chain.

Third, even though China is now the United States' largest agricultural export market, this massive and beneficial trade does not flow as smoothly as it could or should. China remains among the least transparent and predictable of the world's major markets for agricultural products, largely because of unpredictable and problematic interventions in the market by China's regulatory authorities.

Finally, even though the United States continues to enjoy a substantial surplus in trade in services with China, and the market for U.S. service suppliers remains promising, China's discriminatory regulatory processes, informal bans on entry, overly burdensome and capricious licensing and operating requirements, and other similar problems frustrate efforts of foreign suppliers to achieve their full market potential in China.

Going forward, Ambassador Kirk will continue to vigorously pursue increased benefits for U.S. stakeholders in all of these areas, using both bilateral and multilateral engagement, including dispute settlement at the WTO, where appropriate. We are committed to ensuring that the United States fully benefits from China's commitments to trade liberalization under the terms of its accession to the WTO.

TRANSPARENCY AND RULE OF LAW

Let me turn to the important area of transparency. This is one of the core principles of the WTO Agreement, and is reflected throughout China's WTO accession commitments. Transparency permits markets to function effectively and reduces opportunities for officials to engage in trade-distorting practices behind closed doors. China's WTO transparency commitments required a profound historical shift in Chinese policies, and China did make important strides to improve transparency across a wide range of national and provincial authorities following its accession to the WTO. Nevertheless, it appears that China still has more work to do.

Three areas of remaining work stand out. First, China committed to publish all of its trade-related laws, regulations and other measures. While China has complied with this commitment in many respects, it still does not appear that China publishes all its measures. For example, China does not publish measures providing what China calls "internal guidance" to its agencies. These measures can bind agencies just as fully as officially public measures do, and the public should be able to see them. Second, China committed to publish trade-related measures for public comment before implementing them. China has made important improvements in this area over the years, but some agencies continue to promulgate final measures with little or no opportunity for public comment. Third, China committed to all of its trade-related measures available in one or more WTO languages, but it appears that China has made only limited progress in implementing this commitment.

The Administration will continue to monitor China's progress closely in this area and will push China to undertake further necessary steps to improve transparency.

CHINA'S FUTURE WTO PARTICIPATION

China's WTO membership offers an important tool for managing the increasingly complex U.S.China trade relationship. A common WTO "rule book" and an impartial body in Geneva have helped the two sides resolve differences when dialogue fails. The United States has not hesitated to pursue its rights with China through WTO dispute settlement. In the last 3 years alone, the United States has brought five cases to the WTO to address harmful subsidies in wind power, concerns about misuse of trade remedy law, discriminatory barriers in the electronic payments sector, and trade-distortive export restraints on crucial raw materials. These disputes—combined with the enforcement work we pursue in the Joint Commission on Commerce and Trade, the Strategic and Economic Dialogue, and through other trade tools like Special 301—help ensure that U.S. businesses, workers, farmers, ranchers, service suppliers, and consumers derive the full promise of China's WTO membership.

The importance of the WTO to the U.S.-China trade relationship highlights the fact that China itself has a critical stake in participating in, and strengthening, the WTO system. That means, for example, that, at the upcoming WTO ministerial in Geneva, China should join in to help "turn the page" so that WTO Members can solve the Doha Round impasse and implement meaningful trade liberalization and credible trade rules to govern the WTO system in the future.

CONCLUSION

Mr. Chairman, Mr. Co-Chairman and members of the Commission, thank you for providing me with the opportunity to testify. I look forward to your questions.

Testimony of the Honorable Grant D. Aldonas
Before the Congressional-Executive Commission on China
"Ten Years in the WTO: Has China Kept Its Promises?"
December 13, 2011

Mr. Chairman and distinguished members of the Commission, thank you for the opportunity to testify. Having served as Chief International Trade Counsel on the Senate Finance Committee at the time of Congress' consideration of permanent normal trade relations for China, I understand the critical role that the congressional leaders envisioned for the Commission.

I was fortunate, later, as Under Secretary of Commerce for international trade, to serve on the inaugural Commission and participate in its early work. I have enormous respect for the time and commitment you and the Commission's staff have invested in examining China's implementation of its WTO commitments, which remains central to our bilateral trade relationship with China. In my view, these issues also represent a critical determinant of China's own evolution – politically, economically, and socially – in the years to come.

After briefly reviewing some numbers on U.S.-China trade over the past decade and discussing the impact of China's on the WTO, I will return to those issues, particularly the impact of WTO accession on the development of the rule of law in China.

Effect of China's Accession on U.S.-China Bilateral Trade

There are a number of ways one might measure the effect of China's accession to the WTO. The most obvious is the sheer volume of trade that China's accession has encouraged. U.S. exports to China expanded rapidly from a very small base of $16 billion just prior to China's WTO accession to more than $91 billion a decade later in 2010. That amounted to an increase of 468 percent, as compared to a growth of only 55 percent in US exports to all other destinations over the same ten-year period.[1] That trend is continuing, with exports to China rising 32 percent in 2010, which represents faster growth than in any of the other top five U.S. export destinations.[2]

Having said that, our bilateral trade is extremely lopsided, as critics of China's trade and industrial policies have pointed out. Our bilateral trade deficit with China has tripled over the past ten years.[3] According to the Office of the United States Trade Representative ("USTR"), the U.S. trade deficit in goods with China was $273.1 billion in 2010 – roughly a $46 billion (20 percent) increase over 2009.[4] Our bilateral deficit with China accounted for 43 percent of our total deficit in trade in goods last year.[5]

---

[1] U.S.-China Business Council, US Exports to China by State, 2000–10.

[2] Id.

[3] China Data: Trade and Investment Since 2001 in *The China Business Review* (October-December 2011) 34-37.

[4] Office of the United States Trade Representative, *U.S.-China Trade Facts* at

As the chart below highlights, our bilateral trade deficit with China has remained stubbornly high regardless of the broader shifts in both the U.S. and global economy.[6]

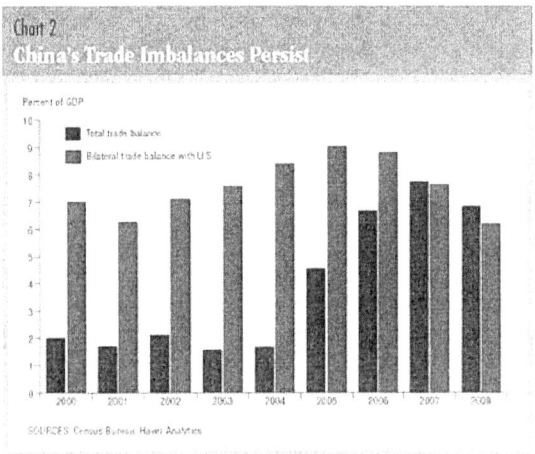

As I discuss below, there are a number of reasons why the deficit is not actually as large as the trade statistics suggest and while, in economic terms, bilateral deficits are far less relevant than our overall current account deficit when thinking about the health of the U.S. economy as a whole, it is still hard to explain the persistence of our deficits with China within the conventional framework of textbook economics.

The question is what to draw from that conclusion. In my own view, there is little that you can draw from the existence of the deficit itself in terms of the specifics of trade policy. Much like legal remedies under domestic law for tort or breach of contract, the tools that either the WTO or domestic law provide are designed to address specific infractions of the rules.

What it points to, instead, is the risk of negotiating solely about border measures and other conventional trade policies or practices, when two countries operate from fundamentally different assumptions about the organization of economic activity, the nature of competition, and the role of the state in the economy in their respective home markets.

---

http://www.ustr.gov/countries-regions/China.

[5] Id.

[6] Wang, J., With Reforms in China, Time May Correct U.S. Current Account Imbalance in *Economic Letter – Insights from the Federal Reserve Bank of Dallas*, Vol. 6, No. 1 (January 2011).

If anything, the past ten years of China's participation in the WTO and the persistence of our trade deficits ought to give us pause before agreeing to allow Russia into the WTO, given the fundamental disjuncture between our assumption of the value of open and contestable markets, whether here at home or globally, and the assumptions that underpin Prime Minster Putin's vision of the Russian economy and the state's role within it.

The traditional arguments in support of free trade, which I fully endorse because of their power to undermine entrenched economic interests that have found a way to vindicate their economic interests through the political process, are ultimately an extension of our collective belief in the value and benefits of expanding human freedom generally. But, that is simply a very different basis on which to organize a society and economy than that which prevails in either China or Russia.

Much of what we see as pathological about China's trade policy is, in my view, an extension of a very different model of organizing its economy. The broader reaches of our trade policy and our international economic strategy have to come to grips with that conflict in a way that calls for better enforcement and new compliance tools simply cannot address.

Lies, Damn Lies, and Statistics

Without defending China's more mercantilist policies, it is still important to put our bilateral deficit in perspective. In part, our bilateral trade deficit with China reflects the structure of trade in a globalized world economy and the erroneous way in which our trade statistics account for the country of origin of goods imported into the United States.

China represents the final assembly point of a regional value chain in Asia that serves world markets, including that of the United States. While the value that China adds in many of the electronic goods it exports to the United States is limited, the WTO rules of origin that govern our trade statistics base the country of origin determination on the final "substantial transformation" of the product.

Substantial transformation is a term of art in the world of customs that attempts to describe a manufacturing processes that results in a shift of a good from one tariff category to another or result in a "new and different article of commerce," depending on the rule applied to the specific good. It is not a measure of the actual value added by that final "substantial transformation," which is what is really relevant when thinking in terms of our import statistics and the extent to which they accurately reflect the reality of global supply chains.

The fact is our rules of origin do not reflect that reality and overstate our both our bilateral trade deficit and our current account deficit in general. The best way to understand that is to think in terms of a specific good, like your cellular telephone.

In the case of Apple's iPhone, for example, the majority of the value in the phone flows from processes that take place in the United States. Another significant share of the value of the phone is made up of parts and components that are manufactured elsewhere in Asia. China serves as the final assembly point (i.e., the location of the final "substantial transformation") and, as a result, the iPhone enters the U.S. market with an origin mark that says "Made in China" and the full value of the phone registers as an import from China for purposes of our trade statistics, despite the fact that roughly 60 percent of the value of the phone is U.S. content and 35 percent of the remaining content comes from destinations other than China.

I do not want to overstate the effect, as substantial as it is in the case of goods like the iPhone. Chinese firms are moving up the value chain, which means that more of the value of the goods that China exports is likely to be produced in China to the extent that trend continues. That is, in fact, the point of China's "indigenous innovation" policy.

In the event, the indigenous innovation policy is likely to fail because it tries to force Chinese firms up the value chain, rather than forcing them to earn it. Equally important, China's rise in the regional value chain will largely come at the expense of other Asian markets, rather than the United States. But, suffice it to say that an increase in Chinese context of what they ship to the United States softens the criticism of our trade statistics that I outlined above.

Again, the question is what lesson to draw from the fact that our statistics fail to capture very much of the reality of global trade, including that part of it which is the U.S.-China bilateral relationship? The answer is that both our current statistics and our current conception of the economic challenges we face are badly out of date and do not form a reasonable guide from which U.S. policymakers can either assess those challenges or design policy options that might advance our interests.

What our approach to rules of origin and the statistics that flow from those rules reflect is an assumption about how industry is organized and how trade is conducted. Our rules reflect the extent to which we conceive of trade in terms of an arm's length sale between independent buyers and sellers in different countries, where the buyers and sellers are highly vertically integrated.

But, the reality of global trade today is anything but that. Well over 50 percent of all global trade takes place within the reach of companies and their overseas affiliates, rather than independent, vertically integrated firms, as was the case in the past. A still bigger share of world trade today takes place within the broader reach of the global supply chains such firms manage.

Our current system of trade statistics, and the deficits that those statistics tend to amplify, simply do not capture much about the relative competitiveness of U.S. firms and U.S. workers in the global economy. They are, in fact, materially misleading.

Seen in that light, one important lesson to draw from the first 10 years of China's participation in the WTO is that globalization has made hash of the way we used to understand the world in economic terms and that we will be doing the American people a terrible disservice if we continue to make trade policy, whether with China or with other trading partners, on the basis of measures that are more relevant to the 19th century, rather than the 21st.

One of the lessons my mother taught me was that the one sure way to get the wrong answer is to ask the wrong question. The way we measure our trade with China amounts to the same thing. It leads us to ask the wrong questions about the relationship and risks leading us to answers that will not fundamentally alter the underlying dynamic in any way that serves our economic interests.

Our Bilateral Trade Deficit with China in a Broader Economic Context

The more important point is not the statistics, however, but the nature of what a bilateral trade or current account deficit means in economic terms. Our current account deficit is a function of our domestic consumption and savings. Our own recent economic history illustrates that fact.

The borrowing binge that brought us the financial crisis was reflected in an extraordinarily low domestic savings rate, with imports making up the difference between what we produced and what we consumed. As U.S. consumers began consuming less and saving more in response to the financial crisis, our current account deficit fell from its high point in 2006 in advance of the crisis, at which point it hit a record 6 percent of GDP, to its current level of roughly 3 percent of GDP, which is about what it was in 2000.

The following chart from a recent report by the Federal Reserve Bank of Dallas illustrates that shift.[7] While our current account deficit persists, it has declined sharply since 2006, as reflected in the decreasing light blue bar below the horizontal line.

---

[7] Id.

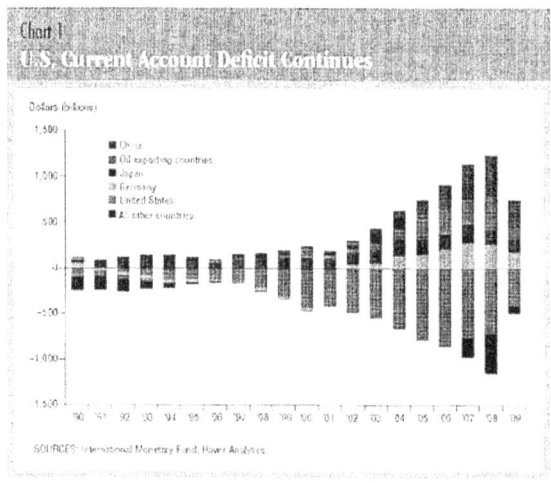

The Commerce Department's preliminary figures for the first half of 2011 indicate that the current account deficit turned down again in the second quarter of this year (from $119 billion in Q1 2011 to $118 billion in Q2), after expanding somewhat from January through March.[8] That suggests that the deficit will remain roughly 3 percent of GDP for all of 2011.

In economic terms, a current account deficit of 3 percent of GDP should not be a major concern from the perspective of our economy's ability to finance the borrowing that the deficit implies, which explains why economists focus on the overall current account deficit, rather than its make up in terms of trade with specific countries, and why they are not particularly concerned with the imbalance in terms of its impact on the prospects for U.S. growth.

I am, nonetheless, less sanguine than many of my friends in the economics profession, largely because the current account deficit has persisted for so long, even in the face of the recent deleveraging by U.S. households, when the standard textbook explanation of the deficit in terms of savings rates should have dictated a far more significant change. I agree that, within the confines of the way economists normally think about the economic effect of the deficit, it is true that our current trade deficit is less troubling than what we saw at its peak in 2006.

But, just like the discussion of our trade statistics above, I doubt whether that captures all that is to be understood from the persistence of the deficit. It seems clear that, if China – and Japan and Germany, as well – had all moved more significantly in

---

[8] Bureau of Economic Analysis, U.S. Department of Commerce, News Release – U.S. International Transactions, Second Quarter 2011, Current Account (September 15, 2011).

rebalancing their economies away from exports toward domestic demand as they promised to do in various G-8 and G-20 meetings, the current account deficit would largely evaporate. It would, at a minimum, serve as less of a drag on our economic growth, and leave room for a greater simulative effect from U.S. exports on the economy and employment opportunities here.

The standard economic case for why deficits do not matter does not really come to grips with that reality. In a dynamic, $14 trillion economy, we are fully capable of bearing the carrying cost of a relatively small current account deficit (at least as a share of GDP), but that does not exclude the possibility that persistent current account deficits may also reflect very differing systems of organizing our economies.

What that means in trade policy terms is complex in practice, but relatively easily stated in principle. Our goal in trade negotiations should be more than simply bargaining for reductions in border measures and other conventional trade barriers. Rather, our goal should be the pursuit of fully open and contestable markets, both because that is the most efficient way to organize economic activity and because it is the only mean of organizing economic activity that is consistent with our underlying belief in the expansion of human freedom.

We ought to bargain with that outcome in mind. The past 10 years of experience with China under the WTO reflects the fact that we did not bargain with that outcome in mind in the 13 long years it took to reach an agreement with the Chinese about their accession to the WTO.

Impact of China's Accession on the WTO

An alternative way of thinking about the effect of China's entry into the WTO is its impact on the organization. There, the record is mixed.

On the one hand, China has proved willing to submit trade disputes to the WTO's dispute settlement procedures and live by the WTO's rulings, even when those rulings went against it. More often, China acted to preempt legal rulings against it by the WTO dispute settlement process and bargained with the United States and other WTO members on a resolution of the specific dispute to avoid that outcome.

The first case brought against China under WTO rules offers a case in point. In 2004, the Bush administration filed the first WTO complaint against China. The U.S. complaint alleged that China had provided preferential treatment for domestic semiconductor producers and that the preferences violated China's national treatment obligations under Article III of the General Agreement on Tariffs and Trade 1994. The European Union, Japan, Mexico and Taiwan all joined in the consultations following the filing of the complaint. In the end, China negotiated with the United States and the other WTO members to eliminate the tax incentives.

In that sense, the WTO dispute settlement system worked as well as it could have. The Chinese tax preferences clearly discriminated against U.S. semiconductors once they entered the Chinese market, which violates Article III. Recognizing that norm, China acted to preempt the need for a definitive ruling and implemented a plan to bring itself into compliance.

On the other hand, China's unwillingness to consider any serious trade liberalization beyond the commitments it made as part of its accession process hampered the effort to negotiate a successful Doha round of WTO negotiations. Both prior to and at the launch of the round in Doha in 2001, the Chinese argued that they had, in effect, already "paid at the office." They wanted the liberalization's agreed to as part of the accession process to count toward their commitments in the Doha round negotiations.

It is genuinely hard to design a stance on negotiations that is more fundamentally inconsistent with both the dynamic that multilateral trade negotiations must foster in order to succeed or to define a stance that is more deeply inconsistent with the basis on which China agreed to accede to the WTO. Accession is a process by which a non-member comes to the table and, through negotiation, offers a package of proposed liberalizations that are equivalent to those already undertaken by the existing members of the organization. In that sense, China's accession was simply bringing China's trade regime into line with the existing commitments and liberalization that other WTO members had already made.

What accession does not do is guarantee that one party will be held harmless in future negotiations. Given that all China had done was accept obligations commensurate with other participants in the trading system, there was no ground to say that China should not be expected to contribute to the process of liberalization going forward, just as was true of every other member of the organization.

China's influence on negotiations within the WTO has taken one other form, which is also negative. To make a multilateral deal that was sufficiently attractive to other trading partners in the organization, developing countries were obliged to come up with offers or a methodology for reaching an agreement with other WTO members that would allow a deal to move forward, even though the obligations they would assume would not be commensurate with those of developed countries like the United States.

In the event, China's accession resulted in fewer offers and greater intransigence from developing country delegations. The reason is that the trade policymakers of any number of poorer developing countries could not contemplate tabling an offer to the United States that WTO rules would require them to "multilateralize" (i.e., they would owe the obligation to all WTO members under Article I of the GATT, its most favored nation clause). Their resistance to such a deal had nothing to do with opening their markets to the United States and everything to do with their unwillingness, in the process, to open their markets to Chinese goods for fear that Chinese imports would swamp their markets and result in the immiseration of any number of people who had previously been employed in competing industries.

In short, China's accession significantly complicated the negotiating dynamic within the WTO and made it more likely, although it was not the sole cause, that the Doha round negotiations would end in failure.

Assessing Implementation and Measuring Compliance

A third way of thinking about China's accession is through the lens of its implementation of its obligations and its record of compliance with WTO rules. As I suggested a decade ago, China made a great effort to implement its WTO obligations in Chinese law in preparation for its accession. By some counts, those efforts included the amendment of well over 2,000 national laws and some 190,000 local laws and regulations.[9]

It is difficult to conceive of a shift our legal regime on that scale. Even the recently passed Dodd-Frank Wall Street Reform and Consumer Protection Act, which created multiple new government agencies, mandated 243 new regulatory projects, required the agencies to conduct 67 studies, and called for 22 periodic reports, pales by comparison. To put it in context, as big a piece of legislation as Dodd-Frank ultimately became, China had to amend more national laws than Dodd-Frank had pages.

Seen in that light, China's implementation of its obligations throughout the Chinese legal system in advance of its accession to ensure, at least as codified, that its laws conformed to its WTO obligations was a remarkable feat.

In my experience, China's efforts went considerably further. Both as a means of easing doubts about WTO and its potential impact on Chinese producers, as well as a means of informing the public about the impending changes that WTO accession would require, the Chinese government undertook a considerable campaign to educate the public about the obligations that China had assumed and the rights that would accrue to China and Chinese producers by virtue of the WTO agreement.

The Shanghai WTO Affairs Consultation Centre offers a case in point. The Shanghai People's Municipal Government created the center to provide a professional, non-government consulting institution to offer legal and policy advice on WTO affairs, as well as WTO-related training.[10] Since its founding, the WTO Centre contributed significantly to the local implementation of China's WTO accession commitments in Shanghai through its advice to both the central and regional governments responsible for various aspects of implementation.[11]

---

[9] Wang, Y., WTO Accession, Globalization, and a Changing China in *The China Business Review* (October-December 2011) 31-33.

[10] Gong, B., Managing the Challenges of WTO Participation: Case Study 11, Shanghai's WTO Affairs Consultation Center: Working Together to Take Advantage of WTO Membership, World Trade Organization.

[11] Id.

The WTO Centre has also played a constructive role in helping resolve disputes at a regional and local level. One early example involved the Centre's discussions with the U.S. Consulate in Shanghai regarding the auction of license plates, which were essential to the purchase and registration of a car.[12] The Consulate staff highlighted the fact that local authorities were operating two separate systems of auctions for license plates, with one set of rules for domestically produced cars and entirely separate and more onerous requirements for auctions involving foreign-made automobiles.

With that information in hand, the Centre entered into negotiations with the Shanghai Municipal Development Planning Commission to establish a single set of rules for the auction of license plates. The ostensible purpose was to "avert a potential trade dispute and protect Shanghai's reputation as a place to do business." The collaboration between the U.S. Consulate and the Centre resulted in changes in the system in a way that brought the auction of licenses into conformity with WTO rules.

Having said that, as early as 2002, we began to see significant departures in Chinese practice from the commitments to which China had agreed in the process of its WTO accession. In its second report to Congress on China's compliance with its WTO obligations, for example, USTR highlighted "a number of systemic concerns" that remained with China's implementation.[13]

A number of the individual actions involved discrimination in rebating value added taxes, one instance of which eventually led to the first WTO case against China, as noted above. The USTR report also highlighted continuing problems in the enforcement of intellectual property rights, despite the fact that the laws on the books had faithfully implemented China's obligations under the WTO Agreement on Trade-Related Aspects of Intellectual Property ("TRIPs"). There were clearly areas, like trading and distribution rights, where China's compliance lagged and there were disputes with China about the exact nature of the obligations regarding the branching of insurance providers in the Chinese market.

But, perhaps the most serious issue, at least in systemic terms, was the halting compliance with the WTO's obligations on transparency, with Chinese agencies soliciting the comments of Chinese industry without even making U.S. and other foreign companies aware of the potential regulatory action, much less aware of an opportunity to offer comment on the proposed rules. In addition, and perhaps not unexpectedly, the overall implementation effort was, according to USTR, "plagued by uncertainty and a lack of uniformity."

It also seemed that the willingness of Chinese officials to resolve implementation issues quickly had begun to wane. Rather than the attitude that informed the resolution of the auction of automobile licenses in Shanghai early on in the process, discussions on compliance began to take on the character of protracted negotiations with progress being

---

[12] Id.

[13] USTR, *2002 Report to Congress on China's WTO Compliance*, December 11, 2002.

made only when the agenda was driven toward some action forcing event, like the advent of a meeting of the Joint Commission on Commerce and Trade.[14]

The slowdown in compliance became a growing concern and culminated in then-USTR, now Senator Rob Portman launching a "top to bottom" review of our trading relationship with China in 2006.[15] The resulting report not only offered a compendium of the challenges that we faced in securing China's compliance with its WTO obligations, it also identified a number of ways in which our enforcement efforts could be strengthened.

But, in re-reading the review in preparation for this hearing, what struck me most were two lines that captured the essence of the problem. There, the report states –

> China's ascendancy as a major international trading partner brings with it certain responsibilities for the maintenance of the multilateral, global trading system. As the size of its market and trade flows have increased, China's constructive participation is increasingly critical to the international regimes governing trade practices – regimes that foster free and open markets, a level playing field, and transparent regulations.[16]

In a nutshell, those two lines capture what is most troubling about China's rise as a trading state. If China's leaders shared that perspective on the role that China should play within an international trade regime that affords China manifold benefits, my instinct is that there would be far less concern in Congress and in the American public about our trade with China and that we would have far greater confidence in the prospects for continuing collaboration going forward.

The Acid Test

In medieval times, there was great concern about various coins in general circulation that purported to be gold. Goldsmiths tested them with nitric acid to be certain that the coins were gold and weighed them to make sure that they were literally worth their weight in gold.

Nearly 10 years ago, while serving on the Commission, I had the opportunity to testify on China's entry into the World Trade Organization ("WTO") and its implementation of its obligations under the WTO. At that time, I emphasized two points. The first was that China's compliance with its WTO obligations should be "the single most important measure of our bilateral relationship" and that "early, transparent, and

---

[14] The General Accounting Office highlighted this perceive slowdown in hits 2008 report to the Chairman of the Senate Finance Committee. See United States Government Accountability Office, *Report to the Chairman, Committee on Finance, U.S. Senate, U.S.-China Trade: USTR's China Compliance Reports and Plans Could Be Improved* (April 2008) ("In addition, our analysis revealed that China's progress in resolving compliance issues appears to be slowing over time, especially since 2003 . . .").

[15] Office of the United States Trade Representative, U.S.-China Trade Relations: Entering a New Phase of Greater Accountability and Enforcement - Top-to-Bottom Review (2006).

[16] Id.

measureable progress on compliance" should be our primary goal. The second point I made, which I believed at the time and still believe, is ultimately the more important of the two, "is the inescapable link between WTO compliance and the development of the rule of law in China."

I still think that the more important measure of whether China's accession to the WTO served our interests and the trading system's interests, as well as China's, depends heavily on the extent to which it fosters a broader respect for the rule of law within China, a far lesser role for the state and the Communist Party in the operation of the Chinese economy, and the steady erosion of the system of guanxi – the connections that dominate both China's politics and its commerce. That to me is the acid test of China's compliance with its WTO obligations.

To understand why that is the case requires a step back from current debates over China's currency policy or the industrial policy it has pursued under the rubric of "indigenous innovation" to look at the broader reach of Chinese history and the organization of Chinese society. It obliges us to understand the tension between two very different views of social and economic relationships that are at play in China and will define its future.

On one hand, there is guanxi, which has formed one of the organizing principles of Chinese society since Confucian times. On the other hand, there is respect for the rule of law, which has actually fostered much of China's economic progress since Deng Xiaoping launched China on the path of economic reform in 1979. China's progress politically, economically and socially will largely be defined by progress it makes from a system based on guanxi toward a system based on the rule of law.

That is not to say that guanxi is necessarily a bad thing. Guanxi describes a reciprocal personal relationship between two people in which one is able to prevail upon another to perform a favor or service. More broadly, *guanxi* refers to the advantages gained from social connections that begin with one's extended family and continue through school friends, colleagues at work, and allies in politics.

In it most positive form, guanxi parallels much of Confucian thought, with its heavy emphasis on reciprocal obligations or *ren*.[17] In that sense, guanxi can strengthen social cohesion. Unfortunately, guanxi can also foster corruption and nepotism and, in the process, undermine or obstruct the development of the rule of law. In that sense, guanxi practice can yield the exact opposite of *ren*.

---

[17] The *Analects*, traditionally attributed to Confucius, captures that notion in a dialog be between Confucius and one of his students. Zi Gong, the student, asks, "Is there one word that may serve as a rule of practice for all one's life?" Confucius, the Master, responds, "Is not reciprocity such a word?" *Analects*, XV.24.

Wholly apart from the benefits to society that may flow from guanxi and its principle of reciprocal obligation, guanxi also represents a rational economic response to what Nobel Laureate Ronald Coase identified as the challenge of overcoming transaction costs in organizing the production of any good or service. Corporations and other forms of business association, in Coase's view, owe their existence to the fact that producing within the structure of a single enterprise, rather than contracting for the same services with independent suppliers in the market, reduces the transaction costs associated with searching for prospective suppliers, bargaining with them for their services, and policing and enforcing the contract against them in event of breach.

In the absence of the rule of law, transaction costs rise significantly because of the difficulty of policing and enforcing any contract with outside parties. The certainty the law provides is, in one sense, a substitute for the assurance an entrepreneur otherwise derives from close family relationships or, in the case of China, guanxi and the network of reciprocal obligations it implies.[18]

Relative to a system without laws, guanxi works efficiently. The opposite, however, is not true. Guanxi is not more efficient than a system of sound laws with adequate processes for enforcement.

As Douglass North, another Nobel Laureate has pointed out, "When transaction costs are significant, then institutions matter. A set of political and economic institutions that provide low-cost transacting makes possible the efficient factor and product markets underlying economic growth."[19] At least in so far as it contributes to economic growth, the rule of law – one of the political and economic institutions to which North refers – trumps the informal networks that either family or a broader network of guanxi provides.

It is currently fashionable to denigrate the "Washington consensus" and to suggest that countries like China, South Korea, Singapore and Taiwan succeeded with heterodox policies that were deeply inconsistent with the market liberalization for which the alleged consensus called.[20] But, the reality is quite different, as North would have predicted.

---

[18] Janet Landa explained it well in saying, "[c]entral to the economics of property rights-public choice theory is the recognition that laws and institutions are important in promoting the efficiency of an economy. One of these institutions is the law of contracts. Contract law, via its role in constraining traders from breach of contract, reduces transaction costs and hence facilitates exchange. But how do traders cope with the problem of contract uncertainty in an environment where the legal framework is nonexistent or poorly developed?" At least in the case of China, the answer, according to Landa, was the development of networks based on guanxi. J. Landa, A Theory of the Ethnically Homogeneous Middleman Group: An Institutional Alternative to Contract Law in *The Journal of Legal Studies*, Vol. 10, No. 2 (June 1981) 349-362.

[19] North, D. C. (1984) 'Transaction Costs, Institutions, and Economic History', *in Journal of Institutional and Theoretical Economics*, vol. 140, pp. 7-17.

[20] John Williamson coined the phrase "Washington consensus" as a means of describing a set of ten policy recommendations that had the support of the International Monetary Fund, the World Bank, and the U.S. Treasury. Those prescriptions for heavily indebted developing countries included, (1) fiscal policy discipline (i.e., avoidance of large fiscal deficits relative to GDP); (2) a shift in public spending away from subsidizing specific industries toward the provision of pro-growth services like primary education, health

Each of the Asian countries that economists like Dani Rodrik of Harvard regularly cite for their success in defiance of the Washington consensus actually share much more with the consensus and with each other in than the critics suggest.

Most importantly, in all of the supposedly heterodox cases, countries relied heavily on the legal institutions that underpin a market economy – private property, freedom of contract, and the enforcement of property and contract rights. Indeed, China's economic success did not really begin until those institutions migrated from special economic zones more deeply into the Chinese economy as a whole.

Understanding that fact is key not only to understanding China's progress, but also to understanding the extent to which that progress is at risk. China's implementation of its WTO obligations helps illuminate the point. The evidence suggests that, in broad terms, "[e]conomic governance in China has become much more routinized and transparent in the last ten years, particularly in response to the requirements placed on China if it wished to become a member of the WTO." [21]

Per Douglass North, that should not surprise us and recent empirical studies reinforce the point. To the extent that guanxi developed as an institution centuries ago in China as a means to foster trade in the absence of a more formal legal system, we should expect that it would give way in the face of China's development of such a system of laws. [22] The reality is that developing and maintaining a guanxi relationship is not cost free. Rather, it is "a time-consuming and expensive endeavor." [23] Reliance on the rule of law is the more efficient, more productive and lower cost option, if that system of laws is available.

Is that system of laws available in China and has the WTO contributed to its development? The answer seems contradictory – it is no and yes. The system of laws that would eliminate the need for guanxi is not yet available, but it is clear that the

---

care, and infrastructure investment; (3) tax reform to broaden the tax base and lower the rates in order to diminish the incentive for tax avoidance; (4) reliance on markets to determine interest rates; (5) flexible exchange rates (largely as a means of avoiding overvaluation and the damaging effect it has on the competitiveness of local industry); (6) trade liberalization, particularly with respect to imports; (7) liberalization of barriers to inward foreign direct investment; (8) privatization of state enterprises; (9) deregulation of markets (i.e., elimination of regulations that impede market entry or restrict competition); and (10) legal security for property rights. The term Washington consensus has, however, taken on a broader and more pejorative meaning largely due to criticisms of the IMF and World Bank by economists like Joseph Stiglitz of Columbia, who dismissed the policy prescriptions as "market fundamentalism."

[21] Smart, A., and J.Y. Hsu, *The Chinese Diaspora, Foreign Investment and Economic Development in China*, The Review of International Affairs, Vol.3, No.4, Summer 2004, 544 – 566.

[22] See, e.g., Carr, J. and J. Landa, The Economics of Symbols, Clan Names, and Religion in *The Journal of Legal Studies*, Vol. 12, No. 1 (Jan., 1983) 135-156; J. Wilson and R. Brennan, Doing Business in China: Is the Importance of Guanxi Diminishing? in *European Business Review*, Vol. 22, Issue No. 6 (2010) 652-665.

[23] Ying Fan, Guanxi's Consequences: Personal Gains at Social Cost, Journal of Business Ethics, Volume 38, Number 4 (July, 2002) 371-380.

process of implementing China's WTO obligations has contributed to greater certainty and transparency in the legal system, to the extent it exists.[24]

What then might alter the situation positively or negatively? On the positive side of the ledger, the United States could lead the way in developing a very different type of trade agreement in its trading relationships elsewhere in Asia – one that focused as much on commitments to the underlying institutions of a market economy as it did on conventional trade barriers. The opportunity exists to build that sort of arrangement in the current negotiation of the Trans-Pacific Partnership, should President Obama choose to use it. All of the countries that are currently a part of those negotiations share a commitment to open and contestable markets, both domestically and internationally.

The value of such an arrangement in the context of our relationship with China is straightforward. China will not be pressured into doing anything that it views as inconsistent with its interests (or, more accurately, that the Communist Party leadership thinks is inconsistent with its continuity in power in Beijing). But, if there is an alternative to investing in China that offers greater certainty and commensurate rewards, it may well be that China cannot afford to remain outside such an arrangement. The door to China's access to such an arrangement should remain open, but only to the extent that it is willing to conform to the underlying assumptions of open and contestable markets domestically, as well as internationally.

Having said that, the far greater likelihood I fear is that the tension between guanxi and the rule of law is already being tipped toward guanxi as a result of the impending generational shift in China's leadership. China is transitioning from a generation that survived the Cultural Revolution and became inherently conservative in its approach to the generation that, as Red Guards, brought China the Cultural Revolution. Their approach is one of greater obeisance to the memory of Mao and less obeisance to the pragmatic approach that informed China's economic rise. That includes less of an inclination to observe the "niceties" of the rule of law, despite the potentially damaging consequences of that approach for China's prosperity and evolution toward a more prosperous and freer society.

While I think the WTO rules have influenced China positively in terms of its legal development, I doubt whether they have the strength or the roots in Chinese society after only 10 years of somewhat halting implementation and observance to offset a more powerful demographic shift that is currently under way in China.

---

[24] As one author put it, "[g]iven the problems of performance and enforcement in the Chinese legal system, guanxi relations play an essential role in providing predictability to legal actors. While the role of guanxi can be limited by formal law and legal processes, the formal legal system [in China] remains incomplete and would have little effect at all were it not for the informal mediating mechanisms such as guanxi relations. Thus, the complementary relationship between guanxi and law will continue to characterize the Chinese legal system for the foreseeable future." See Potter, P., Guanxi and the P.R.C. Legal System: From Contradiction to Complementarity in *Social Connections in China: Institutions, Culture, and the Changing Nature of Guanxi*, T. Gold, et. al. (2000) 183.

When I appeared before this Commission 10 years ago, I made the point that the "[o]bservance of the law in any society must become a habit -- it must be woven into the fabric of social relationships." That does not describe China today, where the ancient role of guanxi remains relatively stronger than the rule of law.

The danger to China, as well as to our trade relationship and the institution of the WTO may well come from the rise of the so-called "princelings" of the ascending generation, who owe far more to guanxi than to the rule of law. I doubt that they can envision China's progress apart from their own. It is exceedingly hard to see how observance of the law becomes a deeply ingrained habit throughout Chinese society if the political leadership of the country does not practice it as well.

Thank you.

WRITTEN STATEMENT OF ALAN H. PRICE[1]
BEFORE THE CONGRESSIONAL-EXECUTIVE COMMISSION ON CHINA
December 13, 2011

I.   INTRODUCTION

In the ten years since it acceded to the World Trade Organization ("WTO"), China has engaged in a consistent pattern of avoiding, delaying, and directly violating its WTO commitments. China's systematic failure to comply with its WTO obligations has adversely impacted the U.S. and global economies and undermines the legitimacy of the international rules-based trading system.

When China formally acceded to the WTO on December 11, 2001, it agreed to be bound by provisions of the existing WTO agreements, in addition to commitments specific to China negotiated in its Protocol of Accession to the WTO ("Accession Protocol"), the accompanying Report of the Working Party on the Accession of China ("Working Party Report"), and the schedule of China's commitments on market access for goods and services. These agreements contain binding obligations on the provision of government subsidies, treatment of state-owned enterprises ("SOEs"), various import and export restrictions, non-discrimination against foreign entities, and many other issues. While China has made some progress toward achieving some of its WTO commitments, many of its obligations remain unfulfilled and, in a number of respects, the Chinese government is moving further away from compliance. In fact, China is increasingly manipulating the WTO system, exploiting loopholes and working around existing rules – in violation of the spirit, if not the letter, of the WTO agreements.

Leading up to China's 2001 accession, many in the United States and around the world believed China's WTO membership would bring it into compliance with an enforceable, rules-based international trading regime, providing substantial benefits for all WTO Member countries. Many expected that China's WTO entry would lead to the opening of Chinese markets to foreign products and investment, by reducing Chinese tariffs and addressing non-tariff trade and investment barriers. In the United States in particular, proponents of Chinese

---

[1] Alan Price is the chair of Wiley Rein LLP's International Trade group, where he heads the firm's antidumping and countervailing duty practice. Mr. Price has more than 25 years of experience representing clients in high-profile, complex international trade regulatory matters, including trade litigation involving public and government relations issues. This testimony represents the personal views of Mr. Price and is not offered on behalf of any client or his firm.

63

WTO membership claimed that it would create U.S. jobs, increase U.S. exports and improve the trade deficit with China. For example, President Clinton claimed in 2000 that China's WTO accession agreement "creates a win-win for both countries."

Unfortunately, because China has substantially failed to comply with many of the commitments it made upon acceding to the WTO, most of these anticipated benefits for the United States have not been realized. China's ongoing trade-distorting practices, including massive subsidies, growing state ownership and control over key segments of the economy, export restrictions on raw materials, and manipulation of its currency, have prevented the flow of U.S. exports to China and the increase in U.S. jobs expected upon China's WTO accession. Moreover, the fact that the world's second largest economy continues to flout many of its WTO commitments and other trade norms serves to undermine the legitimacy of the international rules-based trading system.

II. SINCE ITS ACCESSION, CHINA HAS SYSTEMATICALLY VIOLATED ITS WTO COMMITMENTS

A. The Chinese Government Provides Significant WTO-Inconsistent Subsidies to Its Domestic Industries

Upon its accession to the WTO, China assumed the obligations of the WTO Agreement on Subsidies and Countervailing Measures ("SCM Agreement").[2] In particular, China committed that, by the time of its accession, it would eliminate all subsidies prohibited under Article 3 of the SCM Agreement—specifically, those contingent on export performance and on the use of domestic over imported goods.[3] In addition to export and "local content" subsidies, China agreed not to cause, through the use of any subsidy, (i) injury to the domestic industry of another Member, (ii) the nullification and impairment of benefits accruing directly or indirectly to another Member, or (iii) serious prejudice to the interests of another Member.[4]

[2] WTO Working Party on the Accession of China, *Report of the Working Party on the Accession of China*, WT/ACC/CHN/49 ¶¶ 166-68, 171,174 (Oct. 1, 2001), *available at* http://unpan.org (last visited Sept. 7, 2011) ("Working Party Report"); *see also* World Trade Organization, *Accession of the People's Republic of China Decision of 10 November, 2001*, WT/L/432 ¶ 10.3 (Nov. 23, 2001) ("China Protocol of Accession").

[3] Working Party Report ¶¶ 166-68, 171, 174; China Protocol of Accession ¶ 10.3. *See also* Agreement on Subsidies and Countervailing Measures, Apr. 15, 1994 at Art. 3.1(a)-(b) ("SCM Agreement"), Marrakesh Agreement Establishing the World Trade Organization, Annex 1A, Legal Instruments—Results of the Uruguay Round, 33 I.L.M. 1125 (1994).

[4] SCM Agreement at Art. 5.

Despite these specific commitments, China continues to grant massive subsidies to its domestic industries in violation of its WTO obligations.[5] Over the past year, the Department of Commerce has found in various countervailing duty cases that the Chinese government subsidizes many of its domestic industries, including through the provision of inputs for less than adequate remuneration, direct transfers of government funds, preferential lending through state-owned commercial or policy banks, and preferential tax treatment.[6]

The bulk of the subsidies are granted to SOEs in pillar industries, with the aim of creating large, internationally competitive "national champions." For example, the Chinese government continues to grant massive subsidies to Chinese steel companies, pursuant to government directives and in violation of its WTO commitments. A 2007 report identifies more than $52 billion in subsidies granted to Chinese steel producers.[7] These documented subsidies include $17.3 billion in preferential loans and directed credit, $18.6 billion in equity infusions and/or debt-to-equity swaps, $5.1 billion in land-use discounts, $1.3 billion in government-mandated mergers, and $258.6 million in direct cash grants.[8] These massive government subsidies have helped to create the world's largest steel industry and explain why China's steel exports (particularly exports to the United States) have increased significantly during the past decade. With its total steel production now more than eight times larger than that of the U.S. steel industry, China's exports to the United States and the rest of the world will only increase.[9]

China's most recent national industrial plan, the 12th Five-Year Plan ("FYP"), provides for the continuation of massive subsidies to key industries. The plan, covering the period 2011-2015, mandates subsidies ranging from preferential tax and financing policies to the establishment of "funds" for certain industries.[10] Beneficiaries include small to medium size

[5] *2010 Report to Congress on China's WTO Compliance* at 11, United States Trade Representative Office, Dec. 2010. USTR's 2010 Report to Congress on China's WTO Compliance confirms that "China continues to provide injurious subsidies to its domestic industries."

[6] *See, e.g., Drill Pipe from China*, 76 Fed. Reg. 1,971 (Dep't Commerce Jan. 11, 2011) (final affirmative countervailing duty deter, final affirmative critical circumstances deter.).

[7] *Money for Metals: A Detailed Examination of Chinese Government Subsidies to its Steel Industry*, Wiley Rein LLP, Jul. 2007, *available at* http://www.wileyrein.com/public_document.cfm?id=16051 at iii and 3.

[8] *Id.* at iii-iv.

[9] *See The Reform Myth: How China is Using State Power to Create the World's Dominant Steel Industry*, Wiley Rein LLP, Oct. 2010 ("Reform Myth"), *available at* http://www.wileyrein.com/resources/documents/Reform_Myth.pdf at 2-3.

[10] China's Twelfth Year Plan (2011-2015) at Chapter 1.

65

enterprises ("SMEs"), China's seven strategic and emerging industries (such as clean energy), and the manufacturing sector. The 12th FYP is further demonstration that the Chinese government does not intend to bring its behavior into compliance with its WTO commitments with respect to subsidies in the near future.[11]

B.   The Chinese Government Continues to Heavily Intervene in the Commercial Decisions of Its State-Owned Enterprises, Contrary to Its WTO Commitments

During the course of its accession to the WTO, the Government of China committed that it "would not influence, directly or indirectly, commercial decisions on the part of state-owned or state-invested enterprises."[12] China further agreed to ensure that all state-owned and state-invested enterprises would make purchases and sales "based solely on commercial considerations"[13] and to run its SOEs, including banks, on a commercial basis, making these SOEs "responsible for their own profits and losses."[14] Given the pervasiveness of state ownership in China, these were some of China's most important commitments upon accession.

Despite these clear commitments, the Chinese government continues to exercise considerable government ownership and control over key segments of its economy and continues to heavily intervene in the commercial decisions of its SOEs for the purpose of advancing government aims. As U.S. Ambassador to China Gary Locke recently stated, "China seems to be embracing state capitalism more strongly each year rather than continuing to pursue economic reform goals."[15]

In fact, since its accession to the WTO, the Chinese government has taken a number of legal and administrative measures to increase its ownership and control over its SOEs, in blatant violation of its WTO commitments. For example, in 2003, the Chinese government established

[11] China has also violated its obligation to notify WTO Members of all subsidies it imposes. China did not submit its first subsidies notification until April 2006 - nearly five years after joining the WTO. That subsidies notification, which USTR described as "notably incomplete," covered only the period from 2001 to 2004 and "failed to include any subsidies provided by local and provincial government authorities," which are substantial in China. See Joint Report of the Office of the United States Trade Representative and the U.S. Department of Commerce: *Subsidies Enforcement Annual Joint Report to Congress* (Feb. 2010). On October 21, 2011, more than five and a half years after its first notification, China finally submitted its second subsidies notification to the WTO. Again, the notification lists only central government subsidies and covers the limited time period of 2005 to 2008.

[12] Working Party Report ¶ 46.

[13] Id. ¶ 44.

[14] Id. ¶ 172.

[15] Sophie Leung, *U.S. Troubled By Growing China Intervention in Trade, Locke Says*, Bloomberg (Dec. 5, 2011).

4

the State-owned Assets Supervision and Administration Commission of the State Council ("SASAC") to exercise ownership rights over China's largest SOEs. SASAC enables the Chinese government to exercise considerable control over the commercial decisions of SOEs, including decisions relating to their strategies, management, and investments.[16] China's recently issued 12th FYP further demonstrates the government's continued and substantial involvement in the economy, providing for direct government ownership and control over certain sectors of the economy. The plan explicitly states that one of its goals is to "uphold the basic economic system in which public ownership is the mainstay."[17] Specifically, the plan provides for the following: enhanced government supervision, control, and direction over SOEs;[18] the development of large, internationally competitive national champions (the vast majority of which are SOEs);[19] and increased regulation of state-owned capital and SOEs' financial performance.[20]

The Chinese steel industry provides a particularly compelling example of China's substantial ownership and control over its SOEs. Government ownership and control of the steel industry has grown dramatically since China's accession to the WTO in 2001, and continues to increase, despite its commitments regarding market reforms. Specifically, in 2007, 91 percent of the production of the top 20 steel groups was state-owned and controlled.[21] By the end of 2009, more than 95 percent of the production of those steel groups was subject to some government ownership.[22]

---

[16] *See* 2010 USTR Report to Congress on China's WTO Compliance at 59.

[17] Chapter 45 of Title XI in China's Twelfth Five-Year Plan (Reform in Different Areas, Improving Socialism Institution of Market Economy) ("China's 12th FYP").

[18] China's 12th FYP seeks to "advance the strategic restructuring of the state-owned economy and improve the mechanisms for redirecting investments of state capital to ensure its rational flow." It also seeks to "advance state capital to focus on key fields which involve national security and national economic lifelines" and to "improve the management of state-owned assets and the SOE supervision system." Title XI, Chapter 45 and Title XI at 1 and 2.

[19] China's 12th FYP states that the government will direct and encourage mergers and acquisitions, including by "promot[ing] integration between strong enterprises and trans-regional mergers and acquisitions among superior enterprises to enhance industrial concentration" and "rationally provid[ing] guidance to the merging and reorganization of enterprises." Chapter 9, Title III at sec. 4 and Chapter 4 at 12, October version.

[20] Title VIII, Chapter 32 at 1 and 2. The FYP also states that "the investment behavior of state-owned enterprises should be standardized." Chapter II at 7.

[21] *See Money for Metal: A Detailed Examination of Chinese Government Subsidies to the Steel Industry*, Wiley Rein, LLP, Jul. 2007 ("Money for Metal"), *available at* http://www.wileyrein.com/resources/documents/pu4411.pdf at 8-10.

[22] *See* Reform Myth at 6.

67

The Chinese government also exercises extensive control over its steel-producing SOEs through policy instruments which afford the government substantial leverage to direct the evolution of the industry. In fact, since 2005, the government has issued a number of industrial plans and other policy directives specifically covering the steel industry that have significantly increased government control over the development of the industry, in direct violation of China's WTO commitments.[23] Most recently, China's 12th Five-Year Plan for the Iron and Steel Industry (the "Steel Plan"), issued October 24, 2011, allows the Chinese government to direct and control virtually every aspect of its largely state-owned industry, including resource and equipment utilization, output levels, product quality improvements, technological innovation, and consolidation within the industry. The Steel Plan is yet another example of China intervening heavily in the decision-making of its steel-producing SOEs in a manner inconsistent with its WTO obligations.

China's massive government ownership and control has allowed for the creation of the world's largest steel industry. In fact, China has captured all the world's growth in steel production over the last decade, with Chinese production increasing by almost 350 percent from 2000 to 2009,[24] while production in the rest of the world decreased by 10 percent.[25] This growth has had nothing to do with commercial considerations. In fact, China is critically deficient in many steel-making raw materials and labor is not a major cost factor in today's steel industry. The dramatic increase in China's steel production has occurred despite the fact that the Chinese steel industry has experienced financial returns that are the lowest of those achieved by any other major steel industry around the globe and well below Chinese industry as a whole. As a result, the growth of the Chinese steel industry cannot be explained by market forces. Rather, its tremendous growth has been a result of massive government support for and intervention in its steel-producing SOEs, contrary to its WTO obligations.[26]

---

[23] These plans include the 2005 Steel and Iron Industry Development Policy, the 2009 Steel Adjustment and Revitalization Plan, and the June 2010 State Council Policy, as well as central and provincial government five-year plans. For additional information with respect to these policies, see Reform Myth at 11-17.

[24] See Reform Myth at 2, 4.

[25] Id.

[26] The George W. Bush Administration led significant efforts to eliminate government ownership from the global steel industry in order to reduce market distortions. With the exception of China, these efforts were largely successful. However, as a result of the unprecedented growth of Chinese government steel companies, the percentage of the global steel industry subject to government ownership is currently at its highest levels.

The steel industry is but one example of China's efforts to increase government ownership and control over its key industries so as to achieve governmental, rather than market, aims. The Chinese government, for example, is actively working to "consolidate" the rare earths industry into three primary enterprises so as to enhance its ownership and direction over the industry. Indeed, many of China's key industries have undergone forced consolidation, often in the name of environmental protection. In reality, however, the consolidation is designed to enhance the government's ownership and control over key industries.

C. China Imposes a Variety of Market-Distorting and WTO-Inconsistent Export Restrictions

The GATT 1994 generally prohibits WTO Members from maintaining export restrictions (other than duties, taxes or other charges).[27] As part of its WTO accession, China further agreed to eliminate all taxes and charges on exports other than those listed in Annex 6 to its Accession Protocol or those applied in conformity with Article VIII of the GATT 1994.[28] However, in clear violation of these commitments, China imposes export quotas, export taxes, export licensing regimes, and other measures to limit its exports, including exports of critical raw materials. China also imposes minimum export prices on certain raw materials.

In fact, in July 2011, a WTO dispute settlement panel ruled in a case brought by the United States that China's maintenance of export restrictions on various raw materials (such as bauxite, coke, and zinc) is inconsistent with its WTO obligations and recommended that China come into compliance with its commitments.[29] In particular, China's use of export duties was found to violate its agreement to eliminate all taxes and charges applied to exports, with a few narrowly-delineated exceptions.[30] The WTO panel specifically rejected China's arguments that it was allowed to justify its export taxes as measures necessary to protect human, animal or plant life or health[31] or as measures relating to the conservation of exhaustible natural resources.[32] China appealed the ruling, and an Appellate Body decision is expected in the coming months.

---

[27] GATT Art. XI; Working Party Report ¶¶ 166-68, 171, 174.

[28] Id. See also GATT Art. VIII only permits fees and charges limited to the approximate cost of services rendered and makes clear that any such fees and charges shall not represent an indirect protection to domestic products or a taxation of exports for fiscal purposes. Id. This article is not relevant for the present discussion.

[29] See Panel Report, China – Measures Related to the Exportation of Various Raw Materials, WT/DS394/R, WT/DS395/R, WT/DS398/R (July 5, 2011).

[30] See China Protocol of Accession.

[31] See GATT Art. XX(b).

Despite this ruling and its long-standing commitments, China continues to impose WTO-inconsistent export restrictions on a variety of raw materials, including on rare earth elements. These measures are designed to keep critical raw materials in China and to advantage Chinese producers at the expense of producers around the globe. These export restrictions are also used to entice rare earth-consuming industries to relocate to China. While the environment may be used as an excuse to defend its actions at the WTO, companies have little trouble getting rare earths at lower prices and in sufficient quantities if they relocate production to China. These types of market-distorting practices are contrary to WTO principles.

D. China's Manipulation of Its Currency Constitutes a Violation of Its WTO Commitments

China continues to control the exchange rate between its currency (the "renminbi" or the "yuan") and the U.S. dollar, encouraging a large trade surplus with the United States.[33] Specifically, the Chinese government maintains an exchange rate policy by which it pegs the value of the yuan to a basket of foreign currencies heavily weighed by the U.S. dollar. China's government intervention in the valuation of its currency makes the yuan artificially cheap relative to the dollar, lowering China's cost of production relative to the United States. In this way, the type of currency manipulation practiced by China unfairly benefits its domestic industries and actively promotes the export of Chinese manufactured products.[34]

China's currency undervaluation thus constitutes a countervailable subsidy under the WTO's SCM Agreement, as it constitutes a financial contribution by the Chinese government, which confers a benefit upon its recipient.[35] Moreover, consistent with the WTO ruling in *United States-Tax Treatment for "Foreign Sales Corporations,"* China's currency manipulation appears to be a prohibited export subsidy because it is designed to principally benefit China's exporters.[36] When Chinese producers export their product to the United States, they receive

---

[32] *See* GATT Art. XX(g).

[33] *See* Robert E. Scott, *Growing U.S. Trade Deficit with China Cost 2.8 Million Jobs Between 2001 and 2010*, Economic Policy Institute, Briefing Paper #323 (Sept. 20, 2011) at 4.

[34] Congressional Record-Senate: Currency Exchange Rate Oversight Reform Act of 2011, 157 Cong. Rec. S6020 (Oct. 3, 2011).

[35] *See* SCM Agreement at Art. 1.1.

[36] *United States — Tax Treatment for "Foreign Sales Corporations" - Recourse to Article 21.5 of the DSU by the European Communities*, AB-2001-8, WT/DS108/AB/RW ¶ 119 (Jan. 14, 2002).

payment in U.S. dollars, which they are required to trade for Chinese yuan.[37] Given the Chinese government's manipulation of its exchange rate for purposes of maintaining an undervalued yuan, exporters receive more yuan per dollar than they would receive if China permitted its exchange rate to fluctuate freely. Most estimates place this subsidy at roughly 28.5 percent of the U.S. dollar, even after recent appreciation in the yuan,[38] although some estimates value the subsidy at as much as 50 percent.[39]

In addition to being an impermissible export subsidy, China's currency manipulation is also actionable at the WTO because it nullifies and impairs the benefits accruing to the United States under GATT 1994,[40] and because it frustrates the intent of the WTO agreements, under GATT Art. XV(4).[41] Economists and policymakers alike agree that China's currency policies have enabled it to amass an enormous trade surplus with the United States to the clear detriment of U.S. manufacturers.[42] As Senator Jeff Sessions recently testified:

> So our goods that go there are higher in China than they would be, making the Chinese less able to buy them than otherwise would be the case. The goods they ship to the United States come in cheaper than they otherwise would be, making them more attractive to American consumers. This is a big factor in the surging and huge trade deficit between our countries.[43]

Echoing these sentiments, Senator Harry Reid testified that China's currency undervaluation "hurts our economy and it costs American jobs. In the last decade alone, we have lost more than 1 million American jobs to China because of this trade deficit fueled by currency manipulation."[44]

In fact, the Chinese government openly acknowledges that it undervalues its currency to create jobs and to help its export-based industries. For example, *China Daily*, the government-

[37] *See* 2010 Report to Congress of the U.S.-China Economic and Security Review Commission, 111th Cong., 2d Sess. (Nov. 2010) at 3-4.

[38] Robert E. Scott, *Growing U.S. Trade Deficit with China Cost 2.8 Million Jobs Between 2001 and 2010*, Economic Policy Institute, Briefing Paper #323 (Sept. 20, 2011) at 5.

[39] *See* CRS Report for Congress, *China's Currency: An Analysis of the Economic Issues*, RS21625 (Aug. 3, 2011).

[40] *See* SCM Agreement at Art. 5; GATT Art. XXIII.

[41] *See* GATT Art. XV(4)

[42] *Id.*

[43] Congressional Record-Senate: Currency Exchange Rate Oversight Reform Act of 2011, 157 Cong. Rec. S6020 (Oct. 3, 2011).

[44] *Id.*

71

run newspaper, stated last month that "[i]f the yuan rises too fast, many migrant workers in export enterprises would lose their jobs, for their employers would go bankrupt because of a severe shortage of export orders. This would harm China's consumer market and pose a great challenge for its economy."[45] This demonstrates that China's currency policy is designed to unfairly advantage domestic Chinese industries in world trade to the detriment of economies around the globe, contrary to the WTO's rules-based and non-discriminatory system. As such, China's currency manipulation serves to nullify and impair the anticipated benefits to the U.S. and other global economies from China's WTO accession.[46]

E. The Chinese Government Engages in Various Other Trade-Related Practices Which Violate Its WTO Commitments

- Government Procurement Agreement ("GPA"): China has failed to take the steps necessary to accede to the GPA, although it committed to enter into negotiations to join as part of its WTO accession.[47] China recently submitted its second revised offer for acceding to the GPA negotiations, but the offer fails to cover major segments of the Chinese procurement process, such as coverage of SOEs and an expansion of services coverage.[48] China's membership in the GPA could open up the significant Chinese government procurement market to foreign companies and bring China's domestic procurement regulations into line with international rules.

- Indigenous innovation: Government policies intended to promote "indigenous innovation" are pervasive in China, to the disadvantage of foreign companies and in violation of China's WTO obligations. For example, in its Accession Protocol, China agreed to "eliminate and cease to enforce" mandatory technology transfer requirements made effective through laws, regulations or other measures.[49] However, in many instances, the Chinese government continues to require the transfer of technology as a condition of approval for foreign investment projects in China.[50]

- Intellectual property rights: Upon China's accession to the WTO, it committed to provide effective protection of intellectual property rights and to abide by the WTO's Agreement on Trade-Related Aspects of Intellectual Property Rights ("TRIPS

---

[45] Deng Yuwen, *No Winners in a Trade War*, China Daily, Nov. 15, 2011.

[46] See GATT Art. XXIII.

[47] Working Party Report ¶ 349; China Protocol of Accession ¶ 1.2.

[48] See *New Chinese GPA Offer Covers Some Sub-Central Entities, But Shows Few Other Concessions*, Inside U.S. Trade (Dec. 5, 2011).

[49] China Protocol of Accession ¶ 7.3.

[50] See, e.g., Trade Laws Advisory Group, *China's Laws, Regulations and Practices in the Areas of Technology Transfer, Trade-Related Investment Measures, Subsidies and Intellectual Property Protection Which Raise WTO Compliance Concerns* (Sept. 2007).

72

Agreement").[51] However, as USTR notes, "China has continued to demonstrate little success in actually enforcing its [intellectual property] laws and regulations in the face of the challenges created by widespread counterfeiting, piracy and other forms of infringement."[52]

- Circumvention of U.S. trade orders: There is widespread evidence that Chinese manufacturers whose products are subject to antidumping ("AD") or countervailing duty ("CVD") orders in the United States have attempted to illegally circumvent or evade the payment of duties owed. U.S. steel producers, as well as companies in other industries, have repeatedly brought evidence of China's trade law circumvention to the attention of U.S. Customs and Border Protection ("CBP").[53] Chinese companies circumvent AD and CVD orders through a variety of means, including illegal transshipment of goods through third countries, falsified country of origin markings, undervalued invoices that offset the payment of AD/CVD duties, and the misclassification of goods.[54]

- Transparency issues: Transparency is a core principle throughout the WTO agreements, and many of China's accession commitments involve increasing transparency in China's legal system and in the application of its laws. For example, China agreed to provide a reasonable period for public comment on many new or modified laws and regulations before implementing them.[55] However, despite some improvements in this area, "a significant number of departmental rules are still issued without first having been published for public comment on the State Council's website."[56] Also with regard to notifying the public of new laws and standards, China "still does not appear to notify all new or revised standards, technical regulations and conformity assessment procedures as required by WTO rules."[57]

---

[51] China Protocol of Accession at Annex 1A.

[52] USTR 2010 Report to Congress on China's WTO Compliance (Dec. 2010) at 83.

[53] See, e.g., Statement of Karl G. Glassman, Chief Operating Officer of Leggett & Platt, Before the U.S. Senate Subcommittee on International Trade, Customs, and Global Competitiveness (May 5, 2011) (stating that since 2008 Leggett & Platt had met with or sent CBP information regarding specific evidence of duty evasion on 21 separate occasions).

[54] Staff Report Regarding Duty Evasion: Harming U.S. Industry and American Workers, Prepared for Senator Ron Wyden (Nov. 8, 2010) at 5 ("Staff Report Regarding Duty Evasion").

[55] See USTR 2010 Report to Congress on China's WTO Compliance (Dec. 2010) at 106.

[56] Id. at 107.

[57] Id. at 58.

III. BECAUSE OF CHINA'S TRADE VIOLATIONS, ITS WTO ACCESSION HAS NOT BENEFITED U.S. EXPORTS OR WORKERS AS EXPECTED

A. Because China Has Largely Failed to Fulfill its WTO Obligations, the United States Has Not Realized the Expected Benefits from China's WTO Accession

As one of the largest economies in the world, China's WTO accession was expected to have significant positive economic consequences for the United States and WTO Member countries around the world. Many in the United States expected China's accession to lead to an expansion of U.S. exports to China and greater U.S. investment in China, and to create jobs in the United States. However, as discussed above, China has largely failed to live up to the commitments it made upon accession, depriving the United States and other WTO Member countries of the expected benefits, while China continues to enjoy the advantages of its WTO membership.

For example, U.S. proponents of China's WTO accession argued that it would help balance the U.S.-China trade deficit and create more U.S. jobs by increasing U.S. exports to China's large and growing consumer market. Unfortunately, this has largely failed to occur. In fact, between 2001 and 2010 — China's first decade of WTO membership — the trade deficit with China has soared. The United States trade deficit with China increased in every year since 2001, with the exception of the recession year of 2009.[58] The deficit increased from $84 billion in 2001 to $278 billion in 2010.[59] Last year, China's exports to the United States were more than four times greater in value than U.S. exports to China.[60]

Moreover, according to some estimates, the trade deficit has been responsible for eliminating or displacing 2.8 million U.S. jobs, nearly 70 percent of which were in manufacturing.[61] In total, from China's accession to the WTO in 2001 to 2010, "the increase in U.S.-China trade deficits eliminated or displaced 2,790,100 U.S. jobs," for an average of about 310,000 jobs per year.[62]

---

[58] *See* Robert E. Scott, *Growing U.S. Trade Deficit with China Cost 2.8 Million Jobs Between 2001 and 2010*, Economic Policy Institute, Briefing Paper #323 (Sept. 20, 2011) at 1. "Since China entered the WTO in 2001, this deficit has increased by $19.4 billion per year, on average, or 14.2% per year." *Id.* at 7.

[59] *Id.* at 7.

[60] *Id.* at 5.

[61] *Id.* at 1.

[62] *Id.* at 8.

74

China's failure to abide by its WTO commitments also has had negative consequences for the global trading market as a whole. For example, China's support of its large SOEs and intervention in their commercial decisions forces U.S. and other global companies to compete directly against the Chinese government in the U.S. and global markets, creating significant imbalances that harm U.S. workers and distort the markets in favor of Chinese companies. The imposition of WTO-inconsistent export restrictions on raw materials distorts global trade in those materials, artificially lowering prices for the products within China to the advantage of Chinese producers, and lowering supply and raising prices for the rest of the world's manufacturers. Likewise, the provision of government subsidies to domestic Chinese manufacturers provides those producers with an unfair advantage in global trade.

B. The Chinese Government Retaliates Against U.S. and Other Companies who Express Legitimate Trade-Related Concerns

Not only has the United States been deprived of many of the anticipated benefits of China's WTO accession, when the U.S. government has attempted to use WTO-approved means to bring China into compliance with its obligations, it has been the target of retaliatory actions from China. Individual U.S. companies have also felt the effects of retaliatory Chinese practices. The U.S. and other world governments are often hindered in their attempts to use the WTO dispute settlement system to obtain China's compliance by their own domestic companies, who are hesitant to assist in any U.S. government case or investigation due to legitimate fears of Chinese retaliation. In a November 30, 2011 speech, U.S. Ambassador to the WTO Michael Punke noted the "perception among WTO Members that Chinese government authorities at times use intimidation as a trade tool."[63] Ambassador Punke stated that companies in WTO Member nations report that "Chinese regulatory authorities threaten to withhold necessary approvals or take other retaliatory actions against foreign enterprises if they speak out against problematic Chinese policies or are perceived as responding cooperatively to their governments' efforts to challenge them."[64]

In addition, the Chinese government has taken retaliatory actions on a larger scale, by instituting trade remedy cases in China in response to legitimate trade cases filed against Chinese

[63] *Remarks by United States Ambassador to the World Trade Organization Michael Punke on the China Transitional Review of the Protocol of Accession to the WTO Agreement*, USTR News (Nov. 30, 2011).
[64] *Id.*

13

products abroad. As Ambassador Punke described, "[i]n recent years, a pattern also has seemed to emerge of the Chinese government's reflexive resort to trade actions in response to legitimate actions taken by the United States or other trading partners under their trade remedy laws. This type of conduct is at odds with fundamental principles of the WTO's rules-based system."[65] For example, in apparent response to AD and CVD investigations recently filed in the United States against solar cells and modules from China, the Chinese government immediately instituted its own trade remedy case to investigate subsidies to the U.S. renewable energy industries, including the solar, hydropower, and wind energy industries.[66] Such retaliatory actions can discourage legitimate trade complaints and defeat the purpose of the WTO's dispute settlement system.

IV. CONCLUSION

China's status as the world's second-largest economy makes its failure to live up to many of its WTO obligations — including intentionally flouting certain WTO rules and exploiting loopholes or openings in the WTO system – all the more troubling. Given its size and economic influence, China's refusal to abide by many of its WTO commitments not only harms U.S. and third country economic interests, but threatens to undermine the legitimacy of the WTO and the international rules-based trading system. Indeed, the failures of the Doha round can largely be attributed to China – many developing countries have been unwilling to reduce their tariffs, since China would be the primary beneficiary at the expense of their own industries.

To address these failures, the United States must take a more proactive approach. For instance, the United States should:

- *Aggressively litigate China's violations at the WTO.* The United States should exhibit boldness and leadership in bringing cases to the WTO. The United States should advance aggressive arguments where appropriate (i.e., on currency) and target the most pressing and systemic of problems, instead of engaging on tangential issues. To do this, USTR needs more staff and resources.

- *Stress reciprocity as a guiding principal for all trade and investment issues related to China.* For example, the United States should reassess the access of Chinese SOEs to the U.S. market and takes steps to ensure that China eliminates state support for its "go global" directive.

[65] Id.

[66] See Owen Fletcher, *China to Investigate U.S. Renewable Energy Policies,* The Wall Street Journal (Nov. 25, 2011)

- *Build bilateral and multilateral coalitions with trading partners to limit China's artificial advantages.* In addition to forging better commercial ties with other trading partners, the United States should seek to address the distortions caused by SOEs, export restrictions, currency manipulation and other issues in the context of the Trans-Pacific Partnership agreement, other trade agreements, and international fora.

- *Press for a new, reconfigured round of WTO negotiations.* The new round would be premised in large part on eliminating the loopholes in the existing system that China has used to its advantage. Because China is unlikely to be a willing participant in such negotiations, the United States would likely have to achieve some success with respect to the aforementioned approaches in order to bring China to the negotiation table.

In short, what is needed is a bold, concerted and coordinated effort by the U.S. Congress and Executive branch to send a clear signal to China that it must end its trade-distorting policies and practices and comply with all of its WTO obligations.

PREPARED STATEMENT OF WEI JINGSHENG

DECEMBER 13, 2011

Once the United States granted China PNTR (Permanent Normal Trade Relations) status, China successfully joined the World Trade Organization shortly after. For the past decade, Chinese exports have grown substantially, leading to the rapid growth of its GDP. However, two results came out of this growth. On the U.S. side, the trade deficit with China has rapidly increased, along with a rapid increase in unemployment and the national debt in the United States. Meanwhile, on the Chinese side, the total consumption by the Chinese people did not grow synchronously, nor did imports from the United States.

From another view, in the past 10 years since China entered the WTO the growth of U.S. manufacturing has been slow, and China's consumption has grown slowly as well. A large portion of the growth in both countries was exchanged into cash, which not only had an impact on the financial market but also expanded the wealth gap between rich and poor in both countries. The abnormal development of these two giant economic entities, the United States and China, is the root cause of the global economic recession in recent years.

This deformed economic development originated in unfair trade relations. In other words, the United States and Europe opened their markets to China, while China did not open its market to both the United States and Europe. Meanwhile, the Chinese government has been using unfair methods for competition, especially by way of undervaluing the Chinese currency RMB, etc. Thus, China has been able to rapidly develop its manufacturing industry, while inhibiting the development of the U.S. and European manufacturing industry. At the same time, the Chinese consumer market was not expanded and its imports were not increased synchronously. The profit realized through unfair trading mostly fell into the pockets of multinational corporations and the Chinese government.

When people talk about that wonderful slogan of "free trade", they forget that free trade needs some basic conditions. The domestic economy in China is neither "free trade" nor a "free market". The Chinese Communist government is always the biggest controller of the Chinese market. Regardless of whether you are a foreign company or a Chinese company, you can only obtain market share or market access with the permission of the Chinese government. The condition of this access and share is defined by the Chinese government's needs in international politics, as well as the control of imports of foreign goods into China. The strategic purpose of this control is to keep most of the Chinese domestic market for the Chinese enterprises, especially those state-owned, less efficient businesses that lack competition.

In the past 10 years, the Chinese Communist government continues naked trade protection measures. As China is not a free country both politically and economically, so the government will not unnecessarily use nor is it used to carrying out terms according to the World Trade Organization, or as it promised. Also, because Chinese law is not binding on the Communist government and the ruling party—even if there were a number of WTO conditions absorbed into the Chinese law—they will not be strictly enforced any more than other laws. Chinese laws are understood as tools for the officials: they will be executed if they are considered favorable circumstances for the officials, and will not be executed if they are not favorable. Thus, the WTO simply cannot restrain China's economic behavior; it is impossible to eliminate all forms of trade barriers in China, including the Chinese government's manipulation of the Chinese currency RMB exchange rate, and it is impossible to make China a free trade country.

The result of allowing a country without a free market economy to trade with countries with a free market economy is to let one side hold its trade barriers while the other side is without trade barriers. This way of conducting an international trade is fundamentally unfair. The rules of the WTO are designed for countries with market economies. The current status after China entered WTO for 10 years illustrates that the WTO has neither the ability to cope with a huge non-market economic entity, nor the ability to force China's implementation of WTO norms.

Therefore, there are only two possibilities for changing this massively unfair international trade relation. One is the exclusion of China outside the WTO. However, before one finds a way to exclude it, the other countries must build their own comparable trade barriers to force China into implementing the WTO norms for its own interests. Before China itself establishes a fair legal system, only the loss of interest can force the Chinese government to comply with the principle of fairness. All other treaties or agreements would be something that may or may not be complied with in the legal system in China according to the government's interest, and thus will be invalid.

I hope the U.S. Congress and the U.S. Administration could fully understand the special rules in the Chinese legal system, as well the irregularities of the market caused by China's authoritarian political system. We should not to use the normal way of thinking in a normal society of the United States to understand the Chinese affairs which are totally different.

————

PREPARED STATEMENT OF HON. CHRISTOPHER SMITH, A U.S. REPRESENTATIVE FROM NEW JERSEY; CHAIRMAN, CONGRESSIONAL-EXECUTIVE COMMISSION ON CHINA

DECEMBER 13, 2011

Ten years ago this week, China acceded to the World Trade Organization. Prior to that, the United States granted China permanent normal trade relations. This Commission was formed in that process, with a mandate to monitor human rights and the development of the rule of law or the lack of progress thereof in China.

In 1998, two years before China joined the WTO, I chaired a hearing of the Subcommittee on International Operations and Human Rights of the Committee on International Relations in which I examined whether bringing China into the WTO would improve its human rights record. At the time, I noted reports from the State Department and Amnesty International citing serious problems in several key areas of China's human rights record, such as the imprisonment and abuse of prisoners of conscience, including those who sought genuine, independent representation for China's workers; restrictions on religious freedom; and the implementation of coercive family planning including pervasive forced abortion and coercive organ harvesting; among others.

As a member of the WTO, China has experienced tremendous economic growth and integration into the global economy, but as this Commission's most recent Annual Report documents, China continues to massively violate the basic human rights of its own people and systematically undermine the rule of law. Lawyers and activists who stand up for individuals' rights are detained, often under deplorable conditions—and tortured. Chen Guangcheng, a blind and self-taught legal activist, is imprisoned in his own home. Nobel laureate Liu Xiaobo continues to serve an 11-year prison sentence for peacefully advocating for political reform. Web sites that do not adhere to the government line are shut down. Freedom of religion is denied to those who worship outside state-sanctioned institutions and believers harassed, incarcerated and tortured. Ethnic minorities are persecuted.

This hearing, asking whether China has kept its promises as a member of the WTO, will revisit a hearing the Commission held in June 2002, six months after China joined the WTO. That hearing was titled, "WTO: Will China Keep its Promises? Can it?" There was optimism by some at the time, but even that was tempered by caution. China was liberalizing. It was a vast and promising market and foreign businesses were eager to see the imposition of the WTO's set of rules and principles bring some order to the Chinese investment and legal systems. It seemed at the time that China's leadership envisioned a market economy more similar to ours than to that of a Communist state. However, some people, including me and some of our commissioners, were highly skeptical that China's WTO accession would lead to rule of law in China.

Judging by the experiences of the past 10 years, I think the answer to the first question—whether China will keep its promises—is sadly, no. Arguably, the Chinese people now have more freedom to participate in China's changing economy, but the Chinese government continues to place harsh restrictions on that participation. More Chinese citizens are able to travel, while many dissidents are barred from leaving the country.

The deplorable state of workers' rights in the PRC not only means that Chinese men, women and children in the work force are exploited and put at risk, but also that U.S. workers are severely hurt as well by profoundly unfair advantages that go to those corporations who benefit from China's heinous labor practices. Human rights abuses abroad have the direct consequence of robbing Americans of their jobs and livelihoods here at home.

Charlie Wowkanech, the president of the New Jersey State AFL–CIO, testified at my hearing in 1998 and his words are as true today as then. He said, "Chinese economic policy depends on maintenance of a strategy of aggressive exports and carefully restricted foreign access to its home market. The systematic violation of internationally recognized workers' rights is a strategically necessary component of that policy. Chinese labor activists are regularly jailed, or imprisoned in reeducation camps for advocating free and independent trade unions, for protesting corruption and embezzlement, for insisting that they be paid wages that they are owed, and for talking to journalists about working conditions in China."

On the one hand, the Internet seemingly gives Chinese citizens greater access to information than was possible before, but it is heavily censored, restricting access by Chinese citizens to information and by U.S. companies to the Chinese market. Moreover, the internet has become a ubiquitous, potent weapon of suppression employed with devastating impact.

In 2006 I held the first major hearing on Internet freedom in response to Yahoo!'s turning over the personally identifying information of its e-mail account holder, Shi Tao, to the Chinese government—who tracked him down and sentenced him to 10 years for sending abroad e-mails that revealed the details of Chinese government press controls. At that hearing Yahoo!, Google, Microsoft, and Cisco testified as to what we might ruefully call their "worst practices" of cooperation with the Internet police of totalitarian governments like China's.

Since then China has further transformed from what should have been a freedom plaza to big brother's best friend. The technologies the Chinese government uses to track, monitor, block, filter, trace, remove, attack, hack, and remotely take over Internet activity, content and users has exploded.

Last week I introduced the Global Online Freedom Act, a bill which requires the State Department to beef up its reporting on Internet freedom in the annual Country Report on Human Rights Practices, and to identify by name Internet-restricting countries.

The bill requires Internet companies listed on U.S. stock exchanges to disclose to the Securities and Exchange Commission how they conduct their human rights due diligence, including with regard to the collection and sharing of personally identifiable information with repressive countries, and the steps they take to notify users when they remove content or block access to content.

Finally, in response to many reports that we've all seen in the papers recently of U.S. technology being used to track down or conduct surveillance of activists through the Internet or mobile devices, the bill will prohibit the export of hardware or software that can be used for potentially illicit activities such as surveillance, tracking and blocking to the governments of Internet-restricting countries, including China

Could China have kept it promises? Of course it could have, though doing so would have meant the Communist Party would have had to submit to the rule of law. China faced many challenges when it joined the WTO. However, given its economic success and clout—as well as the immense resources it has poured into the expansion of the state's role in its economy—China certainly could have kept its promises if it wished to do so.

So how is China doing by WTO standards? Awful. China had agreed to abide by the WTO principles of non-discrimination and transparency. However, U.S. exporters face many barriers when trying to sell products to China, starting with customs delays and other problems at the border. Those problems extend into China's markets. Companies in the large and growing state-owned sector [O]operate under a set of policies that favor Chinese producers. Also, it is extremely difficult for our companies to access government procurement.

Some of these barriers are obvious, such as China's indigenous innovation policy, which has created strong incentives to condition market access on the transfer of valuable technology, contrary to WTO rules. Others, such as directed purchasing of Chinese-made products by China's state-owned companies, are harder to prove, notwithstanding China's agreements that state-owned companies would operate on a market basis.

There is no reciprocity, not strictly speaking a WTO requirement, but certainly a principle underlying the WTO. It is much more difficult for American companies to access the Chinese market than it is for Chinese companies to reach buyers in the United States. Even China's Internet censorship serves to keep American products and services out of the Chinese market, by blocking access in China to U.S. Web sites in many cases.

China's record of protection of intellectual property rights, a fundamental WTO obligation, is abysmal. Infringement of our companies' IP leads to lost sales in China, the United States, and other countries; lost royalty payments; and damaged reputations; and presents a risk to consumers here and in China of unwittingly buying counterfeit pharmaceuticals or unsafe fake products.

The level playing field promised as part of China's WTO accession has not arrived. WTO membership has resulted in a massive shift of jobs and wealth from United States to China, which has come at a huge cost to us.

The trade deficit in China's favor his tripled over the past 10 years—in 2010 it was a whopping $273 billion.

It also has come with a cost to the credibility of the WTO, raising the question 'is China killing the WTO?' given China's state capitalism and poor governance.

The impact of China's failure to comply with WTO norms is compounded by the WTO's relative inability to deal effectively with a mercantilist, state-directed economy such as China's. The WTO presupposes transparency and rule of law. These do not exist in China.

The impact of China's failure to comply with WTO norms is compounded by the WTO's relative inability to deal effectively with a mercantilist, state-directed economy such as China's. The WTO presupposes transparency and rule of law. These do not exist in China.

————

PREPARED STATEMENT OF HON. SHERROD BROWN, A U.S. SENATOR FROM OHIO; COCHAIRMAN, CONGRESSIONAL-EXECUTIVE COMMISSION ON CHINA

DECEMBER 13, 2011

Ten years ago this month, China officially joined the World Trade Organization. It was a day of monumental importance to this country, fundamentally changing our relationship with China. It also led to the creation of this Commission, to monitor human rights and rule of law development in China.

Today, we are here to talk about what the last ten years have meant. We've come here to understand whether we are better off, whether China has kept its promises, and where we are headed.

At the time it joined the WTO, China made many promises. Chinese leaders pledged to reduce trade barriers and open up markets. They promised to increase transparency, protect intellectual property rights, and reform their legal system.

China's supporters, many of them here in Congress and in the Administration at the time, argued that WTO membership would bring human rights, freedom, and the rule of law to China.

Those of us on the other side of the spectrum, including my close friend Wei Jingsheng who is here with us today, raised serious doubts about China's WTO membership. We did not prevail.

Yet, after ten years, it's clear that China is not living up to its promises or the unrealistic expectations of its supporters. Far from becoming freer, the Chinese people are burdened with limited or no rights to basic freedoms of speech, religion, and assembly.

And it's getting worse. From the harsh crackdown on human rights lawyers and activists after the "Arab Spring," to the brutal policies in Tibet that have led to a recent wave of self-immolations, China's Communist Party shows no signs of easing its tight grip on the Chinese people.

There's no better example of this than Liu Xiaobo. At this time last year, Liu was being awarded the Nobel Peace Prize. But the dissident writer couldn't travel to Oslo, Norway to receive the award. He was stuck in a Chinese prison, another victim of a system that silences anyone who speaks out for human rights.

At last count, the Commission had documented some 1,500 cases of political prisoners in China. And those are just the ones we know about. These are innocent people like Liu, who are being punished for peacefully exercising their fundamental rights.

Not only did WTO not bring freedom and democracy to China, it didn't bring fair trade either. Instead, China has flouted WTO rules and gamed the system to its advantage.

While China has chosen to comply with some WTO rules, overall, the list of China's WTO violations is a long one.

Rampant intellectual property theft. Massive subsidies for China's exports. Hoarding of rare earths and other raw materials. China has also refused to commit to the WTO's Agreement on Government Procurement.

These violations not only show China's lack of respect for the rule of law. They cost us dearly, in lost American jobs and a stalled economic recovery. U.S. IP-intensive firms alone have lost almost $50 billion to Intellectual Property Right violations, with those same firms reporting that better enforcement could lead to almost one million new U.S. jobs.

Some of the worst violations affect Ohio companies, forced to compete against a country that manipulates its currency and subsidizes its manufacturers.

Given our companies' well-founded fear of retaliation by Chinese regulators and companies if they speak up, we in government must give voice to their concerns.

The most damaging of China's unfair trade practices is currency manipulation. By deliberately holding down the value of its currency to boost exports, China has built the largest trading surplus in history to the detriment of the U.S. and other trading partners.

Currency manipulation provides an unfair subsidy to Chinese exports – of up to 40 percent by the estimate of some economists. It practices the most protectionist policy of any major country since World War II, according to economist C. Fred Bergsten of the Peterson Institute.

Additionally, American manufacturers seeking to sell their products to China— our nation's fastest growing export market— are hit with the same percentage in what amounts to an unfair tariff.

The advantages enjoyed by Chinese manufacturers cost American jobs, and not just jobs in steel, autos, and textiles but jobs in wind, solar, and clean energy sectors critical to our economic recovery.

There's no indication that it will get any better. In fact, China's state-owned sector is actually growing, further skewing the playing field in favor of China's heavily subsidized state-owned enterprises.

With no end in sight, we've got to do something. I applaud the United States Trade Representative's (USTR) more aggressive efforts to challenge China at the WTO on everything from Internet censorship to raw materials. I look forward to hearing from Assistant USTR Claire Reade on her office's plans going forward.

There's still much more we can do. That's why the Senate acted this fall to address currency manipulation. By a resounding vote of 63–35, we passed the Currency Exchange Rate Oversight Reform Act of 2011, legislation I authored with several colleagues. This represents the biggest bipartisan jobs effort Congress has seen this session. I encourage the House to bring the currency bill to a vote.

American workers and American manufacturers can compete with anyone. But they'll never be able to compete on a level playing field as long as we continue to let China do what it wants, without any repercussions.

Over the last 10 years, China has sought to sidestep and reshape the WTO to benefit China, at our expense. That's not competing—that's cheating. We must act now, while we still have a chance.

Thank you.

————

PREPARED STATEMENT OF HON. CARL LEVIN, A U.S. SENATOR FROM MICHIGAN;
MEMBER, CONGRESSIONAL-EXECUTIVE COMMISSION ON CHINA

DECEMBER 13, 2011

I commend the Chairman and Cochairman of the CECC for holding this hearing. Despite nearly 10 years as a member of the WTO, China continues to engage in unfair trade practices. China's joining the WTO offered the promise of a significantly more effective tool for monitoring and changing the trade practices and human rights conditions in China. While it is true that China's being in the WTO obligates China to follow WTO rules, China continues to flout many of the WTO's basic principles in order to promote its domestic manufacturers and exports.

One area of concern I would like the Commission to look at is China's lack of intellectual property rights protections and its failure to act against wide-spread counterfeiting. I am also concerned about the anti-competitive policies China is implementing to favor its domestic renewable energy technology sector and automotive industry.

Earlier this year, the Senate Armed Services Committee, which I chair, began an investigation of counterfeit electronic parts finding their way into the systems that our military uses to defend us. On November 8th, we held our first hearing to look at what our investigation has discovered so far, and what we have found is shocking. There is a flood of counterfeit electronic parts entering the defense supply chain. It is endangering our troops and costing us a fortune. And the overwhelming share of these counterfeits comes from one country: China.

Here is some of what we have found:

- Looking at just a slice of the defense contracting universe, the committee reviewed approximately 1,800 cases of electronic parts suspected to be counterfeit. Those 1,800 involve more than 1 million individual parts. Now, 1 million parts is surely a huge number, but remember, we've only looked at a portion of the defense supply chain. Those 1,800 cases are just the tip of the iceberg.
- Staff selected more than 100 of those cases to trace the suspect counterfeit parts back through the supply chain. In more than 70 percent of cases, the trail led to China, where a brazenly open market in counterfeit electronic parts thrives. In most of the remaining cases, the trail led to known resale points for parts coming from China.

  • We also conducted detailed investigations of how suspect counterfeit parts
from China ended up in three key defense systems. In each case, we traced the
parts through a complex web of subcontractors and suppliers back to Chinese
companies.
  • It is stunning how far Chinese counterfeiters are willing to go. We asked the
Government Accountability Office (GAO), acting undercover, to go online and
buy electronic parts used in military systems. Every single part the GAO has
received so far has been counterfeit. GAO found suppliers who not only sold
them counterfeit parts; suppliers were also willing to sell them parts with nonexistent, made-up part numbers. Every one of the counterfeit parts GAO has
received so far came from China.

At the Committee's November 8th hearing, witnesses told us how counterfeiters
in China remove electronic parts from scrapped computers and other electronic
waste, how they wash the parts in dirty rivers, and dry them in the street. Counterfeiters make this scrap look like new parts and sell them openly in markets in Chinese cities and through the Internet to buyers around the world.

We attempted to send Committee staff to mainland China to see counterfeits markets for themselves. But Chinese authorities impeded our investigation, refusing to
issue visas to our investigators to even enter mainland China. At one point, a Chinese embassy official told staff that the issues we were investigating were "sen-
sitive" and that the investigation could be "damaging" to U.S.-China relations.

They got it backwards. What is damaging to U.S.-China relations is China's refusal to act against brazen counterfeiting.

If China does not act promptly to end counterfeiting, then we will have no choice
but to treat all electronic parts coming in from China—whether for military or civil-
ian use—as suspected counterfeits. That would mean requiring inspection of shipments of Chinese electronic parts to ensure that they are legitimate.

We cannot afford to put our troops at risk by arming them with unreliable weap-
ons or asking them to fly planes with fake parts on them. We cannot afford to spend
needed defense dollars on fake parts. And we cannot allow our national security to
depend on electronic scrap salvaged from electronic trash by counterfeiters in China.

The Chinese government is not acting to stop the flood of counterfeits coming
from their country. But we are. The Department of Defense authorization bill
passed by the Senate contains critical provisions to enhance border inspections of
suspect counterfeit goods and strengthen efforts to detect and avoid counterfeit electronic parts in the defense supply chain. I look forward to those provisions becoming
law.

I am also concerned about the counterfeiting of auto parts, concerns that extend
beyond monetary losses to U.S. firms and directly impact human health and safety.
A counterfeit auto part could be the wheel or the brakes on your car. Since counterfeit parts are often substandard and produced with inferior materials, they put lives
at risk. The Motor & Equipment Manufacturers Association (MEMA) recently has
found that most counterfeits appear to be made in China. For almost 20 years the
United States has been aggressively pressing China to improve its intellectual property protection regime. Yet China continues to be the number one source country
for counterfeit and pirated goods.

There are many other areas of Chinese policy that raise concern and that clearly
violate the spirit and letter of the WTO. We should all be alarmed by China's attempts to dominate the renewable energy industry through measures that discrimi-
nate against foreign manufacturers. China does this by requiring the use of domestic suppliers and production for green and renewable technology. China also has de-
signs to dominate clean car technology. According to the Wall Street Journal, China
is preparing a 10-year plan to turn China into the world's leader in developing and
producing battery-powered cars and hybrids.

At a time when American manufacturers are working hard to compete in the
emerging field of green technologies, China must not be allowed to unfairly or illegally undermine those efforts. The reality is that when American companies do business in the global marketplace, they are not competing against companies overseas;
they are competing against foreign governments that support those companies.

China's trade distorting practices need to be aggressively investigated by the
USTR as we work to hold China to its WTO commitments in international trade.

SUBMISSION FOR THE RECORD

[From the New York Times, December 8, 2011]

CHINA'S 10-YEAR ASCENT TO TRADING POWERHOUSE

(By Keith Bradsher)

HONG KONG—As China heads into a weekend of speeches celebrating its 10 years as an official member of the global trade community, the rest of the world may want to contemplate the exported $49 microwave oven and the imported $85,000 Jeep Grand Cherokee.

Sunday is the 10th anniversary of China's joining the World Trade Organization—a membership that helped turn China into the world's biggest economy after the United States. Companies and consumers worldwide have benefited from China's emergence as a top trading partner. And yet, because of special breaks and loopholes for China when it joined the W.T.O., it still shields its domestic markets from foreign competition much more than any other big nation.

Consider that $49 microwave oven and $85,000 Jeep.

Microwave oven prices have plunged in the West over the past decade, largely because China has combined inexpensive labor, excellent infrastructure and heavy factory investment to produce the ovens and a wide range of other consumer goods for export, making creature comforts more affordable to customers around the world.

Further, W.T.O. rules against protectionism have made it difficult for countries in the West to limit China's sixfold surge in exports during those 10 years, even as the Chinese flood of products has forced factory closings and layoffs elsewhere.

But price tags on imported cars at dealerships in Beijing, Shanghai and other Chinese cities signal how China has continued to protect its home market under the special terms of the W.T.O. agreement it negotiated before joining the trade group.

In the United States, prices for a Detroit-made Jeep Grand Cherokee start at $27,490. But in China, after tariffs and other protective fees, it sells for $85,000 or more. (It's no surprise that Chrysler has sold fewer than 2,500 of them so far this year in China.)

Foreign trading partners often chafe at the way China uses the W.T.O. rules to its advantage.

The Chinese economy's "spectacular rise would not have been possible without the open global trading system that China was able to benefit from during the past 10 years," said Karel de Gucht, the European Union's trade commissioner.

"At the same time," he said, "China is having to increasingly recognize and respect not only the legal responsibilities it now faces as a member of a global rules-based body, but also the W.T.O. 'spirit' of promoting open markets and nondiscriminatory principles."Chinese officials have been effusive in the run-up to their W.T.O. anniversary. "We believe that our 10-year arrangement has been successful—the results of the past 10 years are welcome and a valuable inspiration," Yu Jianhua, China's assistant minister of commerce, said at a news conference last month in Beijing.

The roots of China's economic model trace to the singular terms under which the nation joined the World Trade Organization, which now has 153 members.

Based in Geneva, the group was established in 1995 as the successor to an international framework called the General Agreement on Tariffs and Trade—GATT, as it was known—that had been mapped out in the early years after World War II.

After negotiating for 15 years to be admitted to GATT and then to the W.T.O., China was finally let in after agreeing to accept the W.T.O.'s broad free trade rules. But as all new members do, Beijing also had to negotiate a lengthy document, known as an accession agreement. It spelled out thousands of details tailored to the specifics of the economy of China, which then was still very much a developing country.

The agreement required China to lower its tariffs to levels below those of many other developing countries. But compared with most industrialized countries, China was allowed to impose considerably higher tariffs—tariffs China has retained even as its economy has subsequently grown to No. 2 in the world.

The clearest example of W.T.O. ascendance China-style may be in automobiles. Even though China's auto manufacturing industry and car market are now both the world's largest, China continues to shelter them behind the highest trade barriers of any large industrial economy.

It retains a prohibitive tariff of 25 percent on imported cars, for example, which helps explain why imports represent only 4 percent of the light vehicles sold in

84

China. Japan, by comparison, no longer has any tariffs on imported cars, while South Korea has an 8 percent tariff and the European Union a 10 percent tariff. The United States, meantime, has a tariff of only 2.5 percent for imported cars, minivans and sport utility vehicles.

But the 25 percent tariff is only one reason a Grand Cherokee costs three times as much in Chongqing as in Chicago. In the name of energy conservation, China also assesses a sales tax of up to 40 percent of the vehicle's price based on its engine size. Small, fuel-sipping Chinese cars pay the lowest rate, as little as 1 percent, while gas-guzzlers from the United States and Europe pay the highest rate.

China also collects a 17 percent value-added tax on almost everything sold in the country, whether imported or domestically produced. But like many European nations, China uses a W.T.O. provision that allows the tax to be fully refunded to China's export producers, who often pass along the saving to foreign buyers.

What's more, China limits foreign manufacturers to no more than 50 percent ownership of car assembly plants in China. That special rule, which China managed to negotiate for its W.T.O. accession agreement when its auto industry seemed tiny and vulnerable, has forced multinationals to set up numerous joint ventures in China and to transfer a wide range of technology to those Chinese partners.

China's W.T.O. agreement did open many service sectors of the Chinese economy, like transportation, banking and retailing, to foreign competition. FedEx, for example, has expanded rapidly in China and now has 9,000 employees in the country. The company also relies heavily on American-made Boeing 777–Fs, with mostly American pilots, to ferry an ever-rising tide of Chinese goods to the FedEx hub in Memphis.

And Wal-Mart has been able to open 353 retail stores in China, despite the hostility of many small, local retailers.

China's W.T.O. agreement had some big omissions, including the thorny question of whether to let foreign companies bid on Chinese government projects—an issue that remains unresolved.

China got many of its breaks because the W.T.O. and its members, including the United States, were eager to accept it into the international trade group to encourage Beijing's embrace of capitalism and to make it a more fully vested participant in the global community.

But trade officials say that they never expected all the terms of China's accession agreement to last as long as they have.

Instead, China and other trading nations had expected to reduce trade barriers further in the Doha Round of global trade talks. But the talks dragged on and then effectively collapsed in 2008—despite periodic efforts to revive it, including a meeting of ministers next week in Geneva.

While China is acutely aware of other countries' concerns about its tariffs, it is leery of lowering them unilaterally without concessions from other countries, said He Weiwen, a council member of the China Society for W.T.O. Studies in Beijing.

For the West, the open question is whether China's high tariffs and other market protections will be allowed to remain in place indefinitely. Just as worrisome: a few provisions in the agreement that were meant to blunt the competitive impact of Chinese exports on Western industries are starting to expire. The most notable of these is China's current designation under its W.T.O. agreement as a "nonmarket economy." The label makes it fairly easy for overseas industries to accuse Chinese companies of dumping goods into their markets at prices below cost, and to seek steep tariffs on their shipments.

That is just the sort of accusation, in fact, that American solar panel manufacturers have leveled at China in a trade case pending at the Commerce Department in Washington—a case the American industry is widely expected to win.

But under the W.T.O. agreement, China will automatically be relabeled a market economy in 2016. That status will make it harder for companies in other countries to win antidumping decisions against China—and will probably clear the way for Chinese businesses to further increase their global market share.

Ideally, that could mean a lot more products like $49 microwaves on Western shelves—even if it means a Grand Cherokee from Detroit may never be affordable in China.

○

www.ingramcontent.com/pod-product-compliance
Lightning Source LLC
Chambersburg PA
CBHW082144290526
45794CB00008B/3154